LEON TROTSKY

Leon Trotsky

A Revolutionary's Life

JOSHUA RUBENSTEIN

Yale

UNIVERSITY

PRESS

New Haven and London

Frontispiece: Leon Trotsky in Mexico, c. 1940. Photograph by Alexander H. Buchman.

Published with assistance from the foundation established in memory of Amasa Stone Mather of the Class of 1907, Yale College.

Set in Janson type by Vonda's Comp Services, Morley, Michigan.
Printed in the United States of America by Maple-Vail, York, PA.

Library of Congress Cataloging-in-Publication Dat
Rubenstein, Joshua.
Leon Trotsky / Joshua Rubenstein
p. cm.—(Jewish lives)
Includes bibliographical references and index.
ISBN 978-0-300-13724-8 (cloth : alk. paper)   1. Trotsky, Leon, 1879–1940.
2. Communists—Russia—Biography.   I. Title.
HX312.T75R83 2011
947.084092—dc22
[B]   2010053718

A catalogue record for this book is available from the British Library.

This paper meets the requirements of ANSI/NISO z39.48-1992
(Permanence of Paper).

10 9 8 7 6 5 4 3 2 1

Nothing great has been accomplished in history
without fanaticism.
—Leon Trotsky

CONTENTS

LEON TROTSKY haunts our historical memory. A preeminent revolutionary figure and a masterful writer, Trotsky led an upheaval that helped to define the contours of twentieth-century politics. While still a teenager, he threw himself into the antitsarist underground and from that time on never renounced his commitment to revolution. He organized, wrote, distributed pamphlets and essays, faced Siberian exile, abandoned his first wife and daughters—all for the purpose of opposing a deeply conservative monarch. But when he realized his dream and found himself against all odds and expectations among those in charge of a triumphant revolution, he adopted the very methods of the regime that had once hounded him.

Unlike some of Trotsky's other biographers, most notably Isaac Deutscher, I did not explore his life as an admirer or a follower, nor did I seek to savage him for his personal failings, real or alleged, as I believe Robert Service sought to do in his recent biography. As much as I came to recognize the courage Trotsky later exhibited in opposing Stalin and the profound suffering he and his family endured, I did not find myself attracted to his revolutionary élan when he sought to undermine the Provisional Government in 1917 or to oppose Stalin from his places of exile by resuming his efforts to undermine a dictator. Trotsky fully understood that Stalin was creating a regime that used the veneer of socialism to camouflage its brutal intentions. He also grasped the danger in Stalin's equivocal response to the rise of Hitler when the Kremlin failed to insist that the German Communist Party work together with German Socialists to oppose the Nazis. Trotsky was among the first to foresee that Hitler's triumph would spell disaster for his fellow European Jews and that Stalin would seek an alliance with Hitler if Soviet overtures to the Western democracies led nowhere. But he could never acknowledge that he and Lenin had been responsible for the rejection of democratic values that Stalin soon exploited for his own more sinister purposes. Trotsky asserted that he and Lenin had wanted to fashion a different kind of dictatorship.

History is full of such tragic heroes. They dream of justice and then wreak havoc.

1

The Young Revolutionary

To THE WORLD he will always be known as Leon Trotsky, but he was born Lev Davidovich Bronstein on October 26, 1879, in southern Ukraine, near the city of Kherson. His parents, David and Anna Bronstein, had eight children. Lev was their fifth, the third-oldest of their surviving children; four others died in infancy of diphtheria and scarlet fever. The Bronsteins were not typical Russian Jews. Unlike the majority of the tsar's five million Jews who were compelled to reside in the Pale of Settlement, an area encompassing much of present-day Belarus and Ukraine, Lev's parents lived on a farm, near land that David's father had initially cultivated in the 1850s when he left Poltava to settle among a group of Jewish colonies established by Tsar Alexander I earlier in the century. Most Russian Jews lived in small towns, on the margins of Russian cultural and social life, their day-to-day existence constrained by myriad legal restrictions that reduced them to second-class citizens.

In 1879 Tsar Alexander II sat securely on the throne, but the year marked a dramatic turn in the fate of Russia's Jews and the struggle against the Romanov dynasty. Earlier in his reign, Alexander II had carried out many significant reforms following Russia's defeat in the Crimean War, including the emancipation of the serfs in 1861 and the introduction of laws in the 1850s and 1860s that eased some of the long-standing civil restrictions on Russia's Jews. He ended forced Jewish juvenile conscription; expanded the right of Jews to live closer to the borders of Poland and Bessarabia; broadened opportunities for prosperous Jewish merchants to live in major Russian cities; and, at least under law, permitted Jews with university degrees to pursue government service throughout the Russian Empire.

These changes were not enough to assuage radical opinion, and the Jews remained a vulnerable and persecuted minority. On August 26, 1879, the People's Will, an underground opposition dedicated to the violent overthrow of the monarchy, proclaimed its intention to kill the tsar. And in November, an attempt was made to blow up the royal train. A month later, on December 21, Joseph Vissarionovich Djugashvili, who would adopt the name Stalin as a young revolutionary, came into the world in a remote corner of the Caucasus.

Lev was born into a Russia that continued to be roiled by the "Jewish Question." Seven months before his birth, Russia's Jews were shaken by an unexpected attack. On March 5, 1879, a group of Jews was brought to trial in the town of Kutaisi for the ritual murder of a young peasant girl in Georgia. She had disappeared on Passover Eve in April 1878 and had been found dead two days later. The coroner ruled that she had accidentally drowned, but the police, convinced that the date of her disappearance and unusual wounds on her body and hands were evidence of foul play, arrested nine Jews from a neighboring village. Their trial was the first ritual-murder trial ever held in the Russian Empire, and though the defendants were acquitted, the case provoked intense attention, including a concerted campaign in Russia's extreme right-wing press to lend credibility to the charge.

Fyodor Dostoevsky, who was famous for his sympathy for the downtrodden, nonetheless succumbed to the hysteria surrounding the Kutaisi affair; he was so obsessed with Jews and the "Jewish Question" that he introduced the idea of ritual murder into his final novel, *The Brothers Karamazov*, which he completed in November 1880, a few months before his death. Dostoevsky had also engaged in attacks on Jews in Russia and in Europe generally. Dostoevsky held the Jews responsible for the abuses of capitalism and the menace of socialism, concluding that Russia should not harbor any forgiving sentimentality toward its Jewish minority.

David Bronstein did not allow either antisemitic episodes or the general suspicion about Jews to get in his way. He showed remarkable initiative, buying a farm named Yanovka after the previous owner, then expanding his holdings either by purchase or by indirectly leasing land when renewed restrictions on Jews' owning of land took hold in 1881. Yanovka was remote, fourteen miles from the nearest post office and twenty-two from the railroad station. At one point, Bronstein controlled almost three thousand acres. He owned herds of cattle and sheep, a windmill, and a threshing machine, and he attracted the business of peasants who relied on him to separate and grind their grain. He also owned a brick kiln; the bricks he produced carried an imprint of the family name, and even today buildings in the surrounding area can be found with the word "Bronstein" visible on the walls. Trotsky once ruefully recalled how hard his father worked to enrich himself. "By indefatigable, cruel toil that spared neither himself nor others, and by hoarding every penny, my father rose in the world." But the parents' focus on work took an emotional toll on their children. "The land, the cattle, the poultry, the mill, took all my parents' time; there was none left for us. The seasons succeeded one another, and waves of farm work swept over domestic affection. There was no display of tenderness in our family."

David was illiterate and, according to Trotsky's memoirs, his parents spoke a "broken mixture" of Russian and Ukrainian, leaving Lev at an initial disadvantage at school. And, according to Trotsky, they did not speak Yiddish at a time when 97 percent of Russia's Jews regarded Yiddish as their mother tongue.

This area of Ukraine was still far more Jewish than a casual observer might assume and more Jewish than Trotsky preferred to recall. In his memoirs, he estimated that there were forty Jewish colonies with approximately twenty-five thousand Jewish residents in all. According to Trotsky, his father liked to proclaim his atheism, even to scoff at religion. His mother, although not observant of traditional rituals, preferred to avoid sewing or other small tasks on the Sabbath, or riding into town where other Jews would see her. Trotsky does not say so, but there must have been a sufficiently dense Jewish presence on neighboring farms and in town for her to feel such inhibitions. When the children were young, David and Anna Bronstein marked holidays in a nearby synagogue. But as the family grew more prosperous and the children grew older, there was less and less observance.

When Lev was seven, his parents sent him to the nearby village of Gromokley where he lived with relatives—Uncle Abram and Aunt Rachel—in order to attend his first school, a Jewish *heder*. He studied arithmetic, learned to read Russian, and was expected to study the Bible in the original Hebrew, then translate passages into Yiddish. "I had no intimate friends among my classmates," he recalled, "as I did not speak Yiddish."

Seeing a bit of the broader world brought him into contact with a harsher reality than he had seen at home. Gromokley was located among a group of Jewish and German settlements. One day, Lev witnessed a young woman with a reputation for loose morals being driven out of a Jewish village by a mob berating her with curses. "This biblical scene was engraved on my memory forever," he later wrote. (His Uncle Abram married this same woman several years later.) Lev noticed that the Jewish homes were little more than dilapidated cabins with tattered roofs and scrawny cows in the gardens, while the nearby German settlements were clean and well appointed. The experiment with this school was a failure and Lev returned home within three months. Evidently, his parents' ambivalent Jewish attitudes undermined whatever religious allegiance Lev might have picked up at heder.

Nonetheless, Lev was bright and eager to learn. Back at home, he took to reading whatever books lay about, copying passages into a notebook. He also helped his father with the account ledgers, displaying a talent for numbers that might have taken his life in a different direction from the one fate had in store for him. Spending his time around the farm, he came to know farmhands and peasants. One worker in particular, the mechanic Ivan Grebien, fascinated him. Grebien showed him tools and how the machinery worked. Grebien also had the respect of Lev's parents, who invited their mechanic to take lunch and dinner with the family. In his memoirs, Trotsky made a point of recalling Ivan Grebien as the principal figure of his early childhood. This may have been a sincere claim, but we cannot help but wonder whether it suited Trotsky to place a workingman at the center of his upbringing in a household that was otherwise marked by middle-class, bourgeois values and a father who Trotsky believed was capable of exploiting workers and peasants alike.

The direction of Lev's life changed in 1887 when an older cousin (his mother's nephew), Moisey Shpentzer, came to visit for the summer. Shpentzer was from Odessa. Although he had

5

been barred from the university over a minor political offense, he made a modest living as a journalist and statistician. His wife, Fanny, had a career as headmistress of a secular school for Jewish girls. Lev and Shpentzer took to each other. Shpentzer must have been impressed by this precocious boy, who would not turn nine until October, because he offered to bring Lev to Odessa to continue his education there under his and his wife's protection. In the spring of 1888 Lev traveled two hundred miles by train and steamboat to Odessa.

The Shpentzers turned the unpolished boy into a refined and well-educated young man. Monya, as Lev called him, taught him "how to hold a glass, how to wash, how to pronounce . . . words." Lev began to pay attention to his clothes, adopting a lifelong habit of dressing well. By then, he was assuming the striking physical appearance the world came to recognize: thick, wavy black hair over a high forehead, with pince-nez over blue eyes. The Shpentzers worried that young Lev studied too hard; "I devoured books ravenously and had to be forced to go out for walks," Trotsky recalled of that time. He also enjoyed rocking their new baby girl. As she grew up, it was Lev who "detected her first smile, . . . taught her to walk, and . . . taught her to read." (This girl, under the name Vera Inber, became a well-known Moscow poet.)* The New York radical journalist Max Eastman, who befriended Trotsky in the 1920s, met the Shpentzers and found them to be "kindly, quiet, poised, and intelligent."

Initially, the accommodations were modest; Lev slept behind a curtain in the dining room for four years. But the Shpentzers offered him a home imbued with a passion for literature in a cosmopolitan city that nurtured his curiosity and

---

*In the 1920s, like many other writers and poets, Inber wrote verses in praise of Trotsky. But after his expulsion from the country, she was compelled to denounce him and other opposition figures, even to call for their execution.

imagination. They tutored him in Russian, introduced him to classical European and Russian literature—he enjoyed reading Dickens in particular—and were not afraid to have forbidden books on the shelves, like Leo Tolstoy's play *The Power of Darkness*, which had just been banned by the tsar's censors; Lev heard them discussing the play and then read it on his own.

When it came to politics in the Shpentzers' home, however, "there was dissatisfaction [with the autocracy], but the regime was held to be unshakable. The boldest dreamed of a constitution as possible only after several decades." Shpentzer himself, in Trotsky's memory, held moderately liberal views, "lightly touched by vague socialist sympathies, tinged with Populist and Tolstoyan ideas." The adults remained cautious in front of Lev, avoiding talk of politics "because they were afraid that I might say something censurable at school, and get myself in trouble." For similar reasons, they would not permit him to read newspapers, hoping to shield him from radical ideas.

It was in Odessa that official antisemitism got in Lev's way. In 1887, as part of a broader set of restrictions directed against Jews in the wake of Alexander II's assassination, a new government decree had imposed harsh quotas on Jewish students in secondary school. Depending on the circumstances, Jews could be limited to 10 percent of all pupils. This restriction directly affected Lev. As a Jew, he had to take a competitive examination to enter Saint Paul's *Realschule*, the school picked out for him by the Shpentzers. But hampered by his age—he was a year younger than the other pupils in his grade level—and his lack of formal education, Lev failed the examination and had to spend a year in a special class to prepare for entry.

This incident may well have been the first time that Lev encountered prejudice because of his Jewish origins. But just as in his parents' home, he did not develop an emotional, let alone a spiritual or religious, attachment to being a Jew—Eastman observed that "it was not a thing that entered into his heart as a child"—so this episode of official anti-Jewish discrimination did not reinforce a residual loyalty based on being among the empire's most persecuted. Trotsky was sincere when he wrote in *My Life:* "This national inequality probably was one of the underlying causes of my dissatisfaction with the existing order, but it was lost among all the other phases of social injustice. It never played a leading part—not even a recognized one—in the lists of my grievances."* Other Jewish socialists in his generation remembered their childhoods differently. Both Yuli Martov and Pavel Axelrod, who became close associates of Trotsky's when he first reached London, made a point of recalling the anti-Jewish hatred and discrimination that they faced; Martov, in particular, never forgot the terrible fear he experienced as a child during the Odessa pogrom of May 1881. For Lev, untoward references to his background were "merely another kind of rudeness." Eastman insisted, based on his friendship with Trotsky, that any such incidents "left no traces . . . in his consciousness of himself." Early on, Trotsky came to regard his upbringing within a Jewish family as a simple accident of birth. Estranged from his parents, he distanced himself from their shared Jewish origins. There was no positive content to his Jewish identity.

Although Saint Paul's Realschule had been founded by German Lutherans, it was nonsectarian and accepted a diverse student body. "There was no open baiting of nationalities," Trotsky recalled, and the children were given religious instruction according to the faith of their families. "A good-natured man named Ziegelman instructed the Jewish boys in the Bible and the history of the Jewish people," Trotsky wrote. But "these lessons, conducted in Russian, were never taken seriously by the boys." Lev's father still wanted him to study the

---

*Trotsky preferred a vague euphemism—"national inequality"—in place of explicitly naming the regime's antisemitic prejudice.

Hebrew Bible, "this being one of the marks of his parental vanity." Lev was tutored by a learned, older Jewish man, but the lessons, as Trotsky recalled, over the course of several months "did little to confirm [him] in the ancestral faith." In spite of David Bronstein's avowed atheism, this instruction was probably meant to prepare Lev for his Bar Mitzvah at the age of thirteen, a point Trotsky failed to specify in his memoirs; the ceremony never took place.

Odessa, with its prominent harbor on the Black Sea, was a distinctly cosmopolitan city. Ukrainians, Russians, Jews, Greeks, Armenians, Germans, Italians, and French lived there, along with more exotic communities of Turks, Tatars, Persians, and Syrians. By the 1830s the city had become famous enough that the character of Père Goriot in Honoré de Balzac's novel declares on his deathbed his dream of going to Odessa. For Dostoevsky, Odessa verged on being too cosmopolitan. It was not only "the center of our rampant socialism," as he claimed in a letter in 1878, but "the city of the Yids," as well. As a center for the export of Russian grain, Odessa thrived on commercial relations with Europe, Asia, and the United States.

For Jews, life in Odessa offered entry points into Russian society and culture; the city was probably the most modern place where they could live within the confines of the Pale of Settlement. Here again, as in his years in Yanovka, Lev was living among many Jews. Jewish residents numbered well over 100,000 and made up more than a third of the city's population. Shpentzer's wife directed a secular high school for Jewish girls, while major Yiddish and Hebrew literary figures, like Hayim Nachman Bialik, Saul Tchernikhovsky, Ahad Ha'am, and Simon Dubnow, lived in the city in the final decades of the nineteenth century. None of this touched Lev.

He thrived instead within the broader secular culture of Odessa. Lev discovered opera and the theater and began to write poems and stories. Moisey Shpentzer opened a liberal publishing business, and soon writers and journalists were stopping by the house, thrilling Lev by their presence and their passion for literature. In his eyes, "authors, journalists, and artists always stood for a world which was more attractive than any other, one open only to the elect."

Admitted to Saint Paul's, Lev was quickly recognized as the best student in his class. Moisey Shpentzer eagerly recalled, "No one had to take charge of his training, no one had to worry about his lessons. He always did more than was expected of him." But school had its difficult moments. Lev could be outspoken and in a candid moment once recalled about himself that he was "ambitious, quick-tempered, and probably a hard person to get along with," traits that never left him. He edited a school magazine, but knew enough to stop when a friendly teacher pointed out that such ventures had been expressly forbidden by the Ministry of Education. Another time, in the second grade, Lev joined classmates in booing and hissing an unpopular French teacher. Lev was singled out by cowardly classmates, and the targeted teacher, happy to confirm the identity of the chief miscreant, had Lev expelled for the remainder of the year.

Trotsky drew a telling lesson from this incident. He understood that the school was divided among certain groups of moral categories: "The tale-bearers and the envious at one pole, the frank, courageous boys at the other, and the neutral, vacillating mass in the middle. These three groups," Trotsky wrote in 1929, "never quite disappeared even during the years that followed." The Shpentzers were emotionally supportive, but Lev was anxious about his father's reaction and was relieved—and more than a little surprised—when David Bronstein proved to be understanding and even took pleasure in hearing Lev's impudent whistling, the obnoxious behavior that had so upset the teacher.

Lev was readmitted the following year and quickly regained preeminence among his classmates. But his rebellious nature had not been totally checked. In the fifth grade, a lazy and incompetent teacher of literature named Anton Gamow kept failing to correct the boys' homework. Enraged, Lev and others refused to write new compositions and challenged the teacher to accept his responsibilities. The boys faced punishment for their insolence, but otherwise remained in good standing. Gamow has not been lost to history. His son, George Gamow, was born in Odessa in 1904, studied physics in Saint Petersburg, and defected to Western Europe in the 1930s. He reached the United States and became a widely admired theoretical physicist, famous for his work on cosmology and quantum physics and for his books on science for the general reader.

For Lev, growing into adolescence in the sophisticated and intellectually engaged life of Odessa provoked conflicts with his father. When he went back to the farm during vacations, Lev felt estranged, as if "something new had grown up like a wall between myself and the things bound up with my childhood." David Bronstein could be a harsh man. Trotsky told Max Eastman that his father "had been respected with a good deal of fear by his neighbors." As Lev watched the peasants and his father bickering in the mill over grain and money, he understood that his father did not hesitate to look out for himself.

At times, Lev sensed some kind of injustice unfolding and worried that his father was taking advantage of the less well-off. Lev was attentive to all manner of slights: if his father was too stingy about tipping a porter who carried their luggage, if laborers on the farm received their due but "the terms of employment were always interpreted harshly." One day a cow ran into his father's wheat field. David Bronstein took custody of the animal and vowed to hold it until the owner covered the damages. The peasant objected, begging, his hat in his hand, tears in his eyes, "bent over as though he were a little old woman who needed help." Lev broke down in sorrow, disturbed by the peasant's humiliation and his father's implacable attitude. He was consoled only when his parents assured him that the cow had been returned and its owner absolved of any damages. Trotsky was beginning to grasp the social and economic tensions that played out between his prosperous father and the workers and peasants who depended on him for their livelihood. Lev found himself sympathizing with them and began to feel unease with his father's way of life. Something else mattered more to him. "The instinct of acquisition, the petty-bourgeois outlook and habits of life—from these I sailed away with a mighty push, and did so never to return." That Trotsky liked to recall such incidents may tell us more about his adult sensibility than his actual childhood experience. As Trotsky's most famous biographer, Isaac Deutscher, observed, many people have seen "worse scenes in their childhood without later becoming revolutionaries."

In 1894 Lev was in the sixth grade in Odessa when Tsar Alexander III died on November 1. For the students, "the event seemed tremendous, even incredible, but very distant," Trotsky remembered, "like an earthquake in another country." Alexander III had lived to be only forty-nine, and his son, Nicholas II, had not been adequately prepared to assume the throne. Trotsky was fifteen years old, hundreds of miles from the center of Russian political life. He was barely beginning to feel outrage in the face of autocratic oppression that would, in a few years, merge his fate with that of the tsar whose accession had unexpectedly taken place.

By 1895 Lev had spent seven years at Saint Paul's Real-schule, including the initial year to prepare for admission. Saint Paul's offered only six grades, so Lev needed to choose another high school for a final year of secondary education. To be nearer his parents, Lev left Odessa for Nikolaev, a smaller, more provincial city along the coast of the Black Sea.

Looking back on his teenage years, Trotsky believed that he departed Odessa politically unaware—"vaguely oppositionist," was how he put it. He did not know the name of Friedrich Engels, who died in 1895, and "could hardly say anything definite about Marx." All this changed in 1896, during Lev's final year of school, when he began to question his "place in human society." Living with a family whose children were older than he, Lev was exposed to the passionate arguments of people bent on converting him to their new faith in socialism. He responded with "ironic superiority" to their cajoling. Even the landlady gratefully noted his resistance and held him up to her enthusiastic children as a model of mature judgment.

But then suddenly, as if his earlier resistance had been at least partly founded on an underlying attraction for radical ideas, Lev announced his conversion and proceeded to swing "leftward with such speed that it even frightened some . . . new friends." His life changed abruptly. He neglected his school work, skipped classes, and began to collect "illegal political pamphlets." He "swallowed books" and "began to read newspapers . . . with a political mind." These were the first steps in his political awakening.

Lev also came to know former exiles who were attracting police surveillance, and found himself drawn to his landlady's gardener, a Czech named Franz Shvigovsky, whose interest in politics brought young people and political activists to his modest cabin. Shvigovsky introduced Lev to serious political literature, to the thrill of political debate, and to the often arcane but gripping arguments over the competing claims of the Populist movement and the newly emerging Marxist party of Social Democrats. A member of that circle, Grigory Ziv, in a memoir that is one of the few independent sources of information about Trotsky's life when he was choosing the path of revolution, later recalled that the meetings had a "harmless character." Shvigovsky made everyone feel at home; in the relaxed, informal atmosphere in his garden, they spoke their minds, confident they would be free of police surveillance. So they gathered "like moths to a fire." But their meetings had "a most odious reputation [in Nikolaev] . . . as a center of all sorts of the most terrible conspiracies," according to Ziv. The police dispatched spies who could only report that Shvigovsky was a generous host who liked to serve apples and tea to his guests and engage them in eccentric discussions.

Lev could not conceal the changes in his life from his parents. David Bronstein sometimes visited Nikolaev on business. Once he learned of Lev's new friends and his lack of interest in school, David Bronstein asserted his parental authority, but to no avail. There were "several stormy scenes," with Lev defending the right to follow his own path. He refused his father's material support, not wanting to accept money and the inevitable call for obedience, quit the house where he had been living, and joined Shvigovsky in a larger cottage where the older man had moved. Lev became one of six sharing a communal arrangement.

Lev's political commitment moved fitfully from adolescent curiosity to political action. Initially, he found himself adrift among contending political theories. He studied British thinkers, like the utilitarian philosopher Jeremy Bentham and the liberal John Stuart Mill, whose works were banned from university libraries and courses. He read Nikolai Chernyshevsky's famous book *What Is to Be Done?*, written in a Saint Petersburg prison in 1862. Chernyshevsky was a compelling figure in Russian history. Initially a leader among young, radical idealists, he moved from outspoken criticism of Russian culture to advocating outright revolution. The tsarist regime packed him off to prison, then years of exile in Siberia and cities remote from Moscow and Saint Petersburg. Chernyshevsky died in 1889, not many years before Lev's passion for politics began to take hold; probably, like many of Russia's young radicals, Lev regarded Chernyshevsky as a saint.

But as Lev came to realize, Western thinkers like Mill and Bentham, and even a native Russian writer like Chernyshevsky, for all the romantic ideals attached to his name, were increasingly remote from the controversies arising in the 1890s in the wake of Alexander III's death and the accession of Nicholas II. University students, in particular, were beginning to challenge the autocracy. Asked to take an oath of loyalty to the new tsar, most students in Saint Petersburg, Moscow, and Kiev refused.

Nicholas II was also facing more subversive challenges. Radical young Russians now confronted two competing visions of revolution: the Populists saw the overwhelming majority of the population—the peasants—as the most likely avenue to resistance. They adopted a romantic view of the peasants, particularly after Tsar Alexander II abolished serfdom in 1861. But when the peasants failed to respond to the Populists' dream of overthrowing the monarchy, the Populists turned to acts of terrorism in a vain attempt to eliminate the autocracy.

Marxist thinkers like Georgy Plekhanov urged antitsarist revolutionaries to shift their hopes away from the peasants, to repudiate acts of individual terrorism, and to focus on organizing workers to demand socialism and democracy. It was in the wake of Plekhanov's call to action that Vladimir Ulyanov—Lenin—and other Marxist radicals established the Union of Struggle for the Emancipation of the Working Class, a development that very quickly led to Lenin's arrest in December 1895.

Lev and his circle of friends could not help being influenced by these events, even if they were living far from Russia's urban centers, where revolutionaries like Lenin were hoping to organize. Most of those in Shvigovsky's circle thought of themselves as Populists. Their sympathies were attached to Russia's romantic revolutionaries who believed that only violent attacks on the tsar and his ministers could destroy the autocracy. They had succeeded in killing Alexander II in 1881. Six years later, another group of revolutionaries, including Alexander Ulyanov, Lenin's older brother, plotted to kill Alexander III. But the conspiracy unraveled. Alexander Ulyanov was arrested, then hanged on May 8, 1887.

Lev joined the discussions at Shvigovsky's at an auspicious moment. The group was unevenly divided, with almost everyone arguing in favor of the Populist position, leaving a young woman named Alexandra Sokolovskaya on her own to defend the theories of Karl Marx. Lev impulsively declared himself a Populist and soon led the charge against Sokolovskaya. Ziv recalled Lev's dramatic impact on everyone. "Because of his eminent gifts and talents," Lev was "already attracting the attention of all Franz's visitors." He was "an audacious and determined advocate," relishing a good argument and happy to engage in "merciless sarcasm" about Marxist ideas and any defense Sokolovskaya dared to muster.

Lev was not above abusing her. According to Ziv, Lev came to a New Year's Eve party for 1897 with the startling news that Sokolovskaya's arguments had prevailed; he was now a committed Marxist. His conversion thrilled her. Lev, though, had another surprise. Raising his glass, he turned to Sokolovskaya and stunned the group with a contemptuous tirade: "A curse upon all Marxists," he proclaimed, "and upon those who want to bring dryness and hardness into all the relations of life." Furious and humiliated, Sokolovskaya quit the group, convinced she would never speak with Lev again. She then left Nikolaev altogether. His rude, outspoken style left a vivid impression. "He'll either be a great hero or a great scoundrel," one friend observed. "It could be either one, but for sure he will rise to greatness."

In spite of his sarcastic remarks to Sokolovskaya, Lev, in fact, was moving in the direction of social democracy. Frustration with the tsarist autocracy was spreading among young people and Marxist ideas increasingly inspired their activities. For Lev, it seems likely that he succumbed to the spell of Marxism because it combined a blueprint for action with fierce intellectual debate, the kind of muscular, ideological give-and-take that would characterize his life for decades.

In 1897 Lev finished high school with honors and moved briefly to Odessa, where he lived with an uncle and considered enrolling in the university to study mathematics. But he could not resist the lure of political engagement. In Odessa he "made casual acquaintances among workers, obtained illegal literature, tutored some private pupils, gave surreptitious lectures to the older boys of the Trade School," before taking a steamer back to Nikolaev and to Shvigovsky's garden.

In his memoirs Trotsky recalled a terrible incident from early 1897 that galvanized young people throughout Russia. A young woman student, a political prisoner, burned herself to death in Saint Petersburg's notorious Peter and Paul Fortress. Students protested in the streets, resulting in many arrests and deportations to Siberia. Lev was now determined to move beyond heartfelt arguments over political doctrine. Enraged and enthusiastic, he was ready to take his first concrete steps in defiance of the tsarist regime: to organize workers in Nikolaev. At the time, there were about ten thousand workers and skilled artisans in the city. He adopted his first pseudonym, Lvov, and began to approach workers, inviting them to join small, discreet groups where they could discuss underground political literature that Lev and others secured or produced on their own. He succeeded in bringing together about two hundred workers to what he called the South Russian Workers' Union, drawing on locksmiths, joiners, electricians, seamstresses, and students. Years later, Trotsky recalled his initial success with characteristic enthusiasm. "The workers streamed toward us as if they had been waiting for this," he wrote in his memoirs. "We never sought them out; they looked for us." Alexandra Sokolovskaya was also involved, evidently willing to suspend her bad feelings and work alongside her younger, obnoxious associate.

Lev threw himself into the work. The union needed a newspaper, some kind of broadside, to reinforce its identity and help rally workers to its side. Lev took on the project, calling his newspaper *Nashe Delo* (Our cause). Lacking a typewriter, he carefully "wrote proclamations and articles, and printed them all out in longhand." The effort could require up to two hours for each page. "Sometimes I didn't even unbend my back for a week, cutting my work short only for meetings and study in the groups," he later recalled. Relying on a primitive mimeograph machine donated by a wealthy supporter, he was able to produce two hundred to three hundred copies of each issue.

Lev was establishing a distinct pattern in his life. His revolutionary activity and his professional life as a journalist and editor rested on his steadfast belief in the power of the word. As he grew older and faced wrenching transitions in his life, he would invariably fall back on one fundamental idea: to establish or at least work for a newspaper, clandestine or otherwise, and then pin his hopes on the attention and influence he hoped to generate. In Nikolaev he had the satisfaction of seeing a discernible effect among the city's workers. By revolutionary standards, Lev and his comrades were trying to nurture modest goals among the workers—to insist on higher wages and shorter hours. His pamphlets also covered conditions in the city's shipyards and factories, and abuses by employers and officials.

Grigory Ziv was part of this initiative. Years later, he remembered how Lev was the moving force behind the union. "Our group was the first social democratic organization at Nikolaev," he wrote. "We were so excited by our success that we were in a state . . . of chronic enthusiasm. For the major part of these successes we were undoubtedly indebted to Bronstein, whose energy was inexhaustible and whose many-sided inventiveness and untiring drive knew no bounds." Lev was only eighteen years old. He had still not fully defined himself as a Marxist, but he was already displaying the passionate commitment that marked his life as an adult. He was accepting the need both to study the dynamics of revolution and to pursue revolutionary goals among the workers themselves. For Trotsky, as he explained to young Spanish militants in 1932, "The study of Marxism outside of revolutionary struggle can form library rats, but not revolutionaries. Participation in the revolutionary struggle without the study of Marxism will inevitably be filled with hazards, be less confident, and turn out to be half-blind."

Lev's success as an organizer drew the attention of more than workers. The police also began to take notice, although they took a while to realize that a small group of young activists led by a teenager was responsible for so much unwanted commotion. The arrests began in January 1898. Most members of the group were detained in Nikolaev, but Lev, fearing arrest, sought refuge in the countryside where Shvigovsky was staying. The police took them both away on January 28. They transferred Lev to a prison in Nikolaev—his first of twenty prisons, as he liked to say—then to another jail in Kherson, where he remained for several months.

Tsarist prisons were miserable places. A harsh regimen compounded the physical conditions. Officials had come to understand that Lev was the ringleader and, determined to break his will, subjected him to unusual pressure. He was kept in isolation in a small, cold, vermin-riddled cell. He was given a straw mattress to sleep on, but it was removed at dawn so that he could not comfortably sit down during the day. He was not allowed into the prison yard for exercise, nor could he receive a book, a newspaper, soap, or clean underwear. He was neither interrogated nor told the charges against him. Other imprisoned members of the union fared even worse. Subjected to torture, they committed suicide, went insane, or agreed to inform on their comrades in exchange for better treatment. But Lev persevered, in spite of the severe loneliness. "The solitude was unbroken, worse than any I ever experienced afterward," he recalled about that time. To relieve the pressure, he walked continually in the cell, "taking one thousand, one hundred and eleven steps on the diagonal." At some point prison officials backed down, allowing his mother, who no doubt had to bribe her way in, to bring him soap, linen, and fruit.

By the summer of 1898 Lev was taken to a prison in Odessa, where, once again, he faced solitary confinement, but at least had the satisfaction of undergoing interrogation for the first time. Through the prison grapevine, he learned about the founding congress of the Social Democratic Party in Minsk; in spite of its august title, the "congress" comprised a meeting of nine delegates, who were almost all arrested within weeks—hardly an auspicious beginning for a faction of that same political party that seized power nineteen years later in the name of Communism.

With time on his hands and facing a less severe prison regimen, Lev took to reading. The prison library offered only religious literature. To broaden his knowledge of foreign languages, Lev read the Bible in English, French, German, and Italian. Able to receive books from the outside, he read the works of Charles Darwin, which reinforced his commitment to atheism. He also wrote literary essays, including a history of Freemasonry and another on the role of the individual in history.

It took nearly two full years before Lev learned of his ultimate punishment: he and three others from the union were to be deported to Siberia for four years. It was an administrative punishment; there was no trial. From Odessa, they were brought to Moscow and made to wait another six months in a transit prison. It was here that Lev first heard about Vladimir Lenin and began to read serious works of Marxist thought. He also began a lifelong fascination with Ferdinand LaSalle. The founder of the German Social Democratic Party, LaSalle, like Lev, had been born to a middle-class Jewish family. Like the man Lev would become, LaSalle was famous for his abilities as an orator and an organizer. Each relied on a charismatic personality to arouse the loyalty of crowds. And both abandoned their Jewish origins, replacing the faith of their fathers with a heartfelt and all-encompassing belief in revolutionary socialism.

Lev also renewed contact with Alexandra Sokolovskaya. Facing Siberian exile, they decided to get married. Lev's father strenuously objected, convinced that this older woman was responsible for leading Lev astray. But Lev prevailed. The wedding took place in the spring of 1900, with a rabbi presiding in Lev's cell. It would be natural to wonder whether the impulse behind this marriage was genuine. Political prisoners often married each other because it conferred the right to face deportation together and thereby avoid complete isolation. Lenin and Nadezhda Krupskaya, for example, had been deported to separate cities in 1897 but then arranged permission to be married, affording her the right to join him in a small town in central Siberia. As for Lev and Sokolovskaya, the initial tension between them may well have reflected more than an ideological disagreement. Lev had "raged and thundered" to overcome his father's opposition. Once married, they were sent off in a large group of convicts. Their journey to Siberia lasted about three months, with stops in transit prisons before reaching the Lena River, where they were put on a barge with a group of soldiers and, after three more weeks of slowly drifting down the river, reached the village of Ust-Kot.

It was a desolate place, a hundred peasant huts surrounded by mud in the spring and fall, with annoying midges besetting everyone in the summer and temperatures far below freezing in the winter. Lev studied Marx, "brushing cockroaches off the pages." Soon after reaching Ust-Kot, he also began to write for *Vostochnoe Obozrenie* (The eastern review), a newspaper in Irkutsk. His articles began to appear on a regular basis. Lev proved to be far more than a village correspondent. He wrote about public questions and increasingly devoted himself to literary criticism, a form that made it easier to slip ideas past the censors. He wrote about Russia's classic authors and, being a voracious reader, completed articles about Ibsen, Hauptmann, and Nietzsche, de Maupassant, Andreyev, and Gorky. Living in exile and intent on continuing his involvement in revolution, Lev adopted another pen name—Antid Oto—based on a word he found in the Italian dictionary.

The Lena River acted as a tool of communication, with political exiles of all stripes navigating their way north and south to seek companionship and share news about politics and revolution. Lev met Felix Dzherzhinsky, later the first leader of the dreaded Cheka (the Bolshevik secret police), and Mikhail Uritsky, who became chairman of the Petrograd Cheka. The exiles debated among themselves, feeling the momentum of revolution move away from Populism toward Marxism. They knew about acts of terrorism: both the minister of education and the minister of the interior were shot in those years by members of the Socialist Revolutionary Party. Lev opposed such acts of terrorism. "Our task is not the assassination of the tsar's ministers, but the revolutionary overthrow of tsarism," he insisted.

Observing how the concerted powers of the regime could oppress society at large and underground activists like himself, Lev argued in an essay that it was time to create a centralized party that could coordinate revolutionary activity. Lev was not alone in advocating this idea. In the summer of 1902 he received his first copy of *Iskra* (Spark), a Marxist newspaper published by Russian Social Democrats in Zurich; Vladimir Lenin was among them. Lenin had been released from exile in 1900 and soon received permission to leave Russia for Europe, where the regime assumed that he would cause less trouble. Lev also received a copy of Lenin's book *What Is to Be Done?* (named for Chernyshevsky's earlier work). Lenin, in both this book and in *Iskra*, was trying to rally followers to the cause of

Marxism under the banner of a disciplined, professional party of revolutionaries. (*Iskra* was more than a newspaper; it was the central organizing mechanism to help lead the broader Social Democratic movement.) Mesmerized, Lev grew determined to join Lenin in Europe.

From the perspective of history, it is natural to think that the tragedy of Bolshevism begins here, that creating this kind of party was the germ that led to horrors under Lenin, Trotsky, and Stalin. But given the prevailing conditions under the tsar, it might well have been the only way a socialist movement could challenge the autocracy. It was one thing, however, to challenge power in a clandestine manner under a ruthless monarch. It became quite another to govern with the same single-minded purpose.

By the time Lev made plans to reach Europe, he and Alexandra Sokolovskaya had two daughters, Zinaida and Nina, the latter only four months old. Despite how hard it would be to raise the girls alone under the stark conditions of Siberian exile, Sokolovskaya understood Lev's need to rejoin the struggle. Sokolovskaya, who rarely saw Trotsky after that, always maintained a respectful loyalty to him. She never renounced him in the face of Stalinist repression and eventually paid with her life for that devotion.

Lev chose to leave at a time when "there was an epidemic of escapes," so many that the exiles had to adjust their pace in order to avoid overwhelming the system. Lev had to leave before autumn, when the roads became impassable. That August, he and a second exile hid themselves under hay in the back of a cart until they reached a railway station. His friends from Irkutsk provided him with respectable clothing. And he carried a false passport "made out in the name of Trotsky, which I wrote in at random, without even imaging that it would become my name for the rest of my life." Trotsky had been the name of one of his jailers in Odessa; it is possible that the name's similarity to the German word for "stubborn" (*trotzig*) was what attracted him. The remainder of his escape "proved to be quite without romantic glamour." When he reached Samara, local Social Democrats, who were allied with Lenin and *Iskra*, took him in, gave him another pseudonym—*Pero*, or the pen—then asked him to visit major cities in Ukraine to meet with other revolutionaries. The trip proved to be fruitless; what people he found were ineffectual. By then, Lenin had learned of him and his literary and intellectual talents. Straightaway he sent an urgent message that Trotsky should report to *Iskra* headquarters in Europe.

With the help of the *Iskra* organization, Trotsky smuggled himself out of Russia into Austria. He reached Vienna and was welcomed by Dr. Victor Adler, the leader of the Austrian Social Democratic Party. Trotsky convinced Adler that "the interests of the Russian revolution demanded [his] immediate presence in Zurich," where Lenin awaited his arrival. Lenin, though, was now in London. With Adler's assistance, Trotsky reached England, by way of Zurich and Paris, in October 1902. It was early morning when he knocked three times on the door of Lenin's apartment, as he had been instructed to do. Lenin was still in bed when Nadezhda Krupskaya opened the door and warmly greeted the young man. "The 'pen' has arrived," she announced to Lenin. Thus Lenin and Trotsky met. Together, fifteen years later, they led an armed uprising in Petrograd.

2

The Revolution of 1905

LENIN WAS ALWAYS a good listener and Trotsky had a lot to say. Although he was young and untested, Trotsky had a reputation as a writer and organizer that preceded him into Europe. Lenin and his fellow *Iskra* editors followed events in Russia as best they could, reading newspapers and underground literature, eager to keep their fingers on the pulse of revolution and reaction. While Trotsky's experiences in Nikolaev and Odessa amounted to a small-bore adventure, they demonstrated to Lenin how Marxist ideas were percolating throughout the empire, inspiring articulate and committed young people who might someday, who *could* someday, make the revolution succeed.

Later on the day they met, Lenin introduced Trotsky to the other members of the *Iskra* editorial board. They were all veteran revolutionaries who had endured arrest, prisons, and internal exile and were now unable to return safely to Russia.

Among them were Vera Zasulich and Yuli Martov, who welcomed Trotsky to their rooming house. Zasulich, the only woman among the editors, had made a name for herself in 1878 when she fired a shot at Fyodor Trepov, the governor general of Saint Petersburg. Caught in the act, Zasulich was tried before a jury, which acquitted her; she then escaped abroad. Yuli Martov, who was descended from Hebrew scholars and whose real name was Tsedarbaum, was a close friend of Lenin's. A leading intellectual among Russian Marxists, Martov had met Lenin in Saint Petersburg in 1895. Lenin was impressed with Martov's insistence on the need to broaden Marxist activity beyond explicating the works of Karl Marx. They needed to organize real workers, the very proletariat on whose behalf they were agitating. He and Lenin helped to establish the Union of Struggle for the Emancipation of Workers. This led to their arrest. In 1897 Martov played a role in the establishment of the Bund, a popular Jewish socialist party. For a time he believed that Jews needed to organize exclusively among themselves, an idea he later abandoned.

The other *Iskra* members were Georgy Plekhanov, the legendary founder of Russian Marxism, who was the oldest of the group; Pavel Axelrod, like Trotsky a Jew from southern Ukraine, who divided his time between London and Zurich; and Alexander Potresov, a close associate of Lenin's from Saint Petersburg.

As this small but influential group demonstrated, many revolutionaries were Jews—a fact that at least some tsarist officials acknowledged was their own doing: the regime's antisemitic policies had pushed these young people to the revolutionary cause. No less a figure than Count Sergei Witte, the tsarist minister who was among the most forward-looking of Russian officials, acknowledged in his memoirs that Jews came to prominence in the revolutionary movement because of "their lack of rights, as well as by the pogroms that were not only tolerated by the government but in fact organized by it." Lenin, too, had a Jewish maternal great-grandfather named Moshko Blank, but it seems unlikely that Lenin, his allies, or his enemies knew it at the time.

Trotsky's arrival in London was useful for Lenin. The *Iskra* editors were divided among themselves. As there were six, it could be difficult to establish a majority. This frustrated Lenin; he wanted Trotsky, with his natural abilities and youthful energy, to join the board, hoping that his recruit would vote alongside him as disputes arose. Plekhanov balked; he may have been jealous over a younger man's entry into the fold. Plekhanov was already feeling threatened by Lenin's determined ascendancy among the editors, and Trotsky was nearly ten years younger than Lenin. Plekhanov also felt uncomfortable with having yet another Jew in the group. The other editors liked Trotsky and wanted his involvement. In the face of Plekhanov's objections, they did not second Trotsky onto the board, but they welcomed his articles.

Trotsky quickly made his mark, impressing Lenin as a man of "exceptional abilities." At Lenin's urging, he delivered speeches in London, Brussels, Liège, and Paris. During his visit to France, he met his second wife, Natalia Sedova, who was studying art at the Sorbonne and had the assignment of welcoming political émigrés like Trotsky to Paris, finding them rooms and pointing out cheap restaurants. Trotsky was drawn to her as soon as he saw her come down the stairs in his modest hotel. Although he never legally divorced Alexandra Sokolovskaya, Natalia Sedova became his life companion and the mother of his two sons. Max Eastman met her in Moscow in the 1920s and imagined her two decades earlier as a "strong-hearted quiet girl with high cheekbones and eyes a little sad— a girl of noble birth, who had been a rebel since childhood." She had been expelled from a girls' boarding school for persuading her class to avoid chapel services and to read revolutionary literature rather than the Bible. She then made her way to Geneva and joined up with *Iskra* activists. According to Eastman, by the time Sedova met Trotsky in Paris, she had made at least one clandestine trip into Russia to deliver illegal literature.

Trotsky also contributed to *Iskra* on a wide range of topics. He wrote about the two hundredth anniversary of Tsar Peter the Great's notorious Schlüsselburg fortress, where Lenin's older brother Alexander had been held before his execution. The prison was for Trotsky a symbol of the corruption and illegitimate violence of the autocracy. But even as he castigated the regime, he expressed contempt for its liberal critics. Trotsky had no patience with fainthearted liberals, "that lawful opposition to a lawless government." Another article was about the tsar's plan to compel the people of Finland to adopt the Russian language. Finland was a semiautonomous province of the Russian Empire and naturally enough protective of its cultural and political autonomy. In one piece Trotsky denounced the expulsion of Maxim Gorky from the Imperial Academy, in another he dismissed the newly formed Socialist Revolutionary Party, pointing to its advocacy of terrorism as a futile substitute for organizing the proletariat—the only solution to Russia's political impasse.

During Trotsky's first months in Western Europe, in early April 1903, terrible news emerged from Russia about a pogrom directed against the Jews of Kishinev, the capital of the Bessarabian province of Moldova (today the city is also known as Chişinău). A Christian Russian boy was found murdered twenty-five miles north of Kishinev, in the city of Dubossary. Local antisemitic newspapers fabricated the claim that the boy had been murdered by the Jews in order to use his blood to bake matzoh for the impending Passover holiday—the blood libel that had plagued Jewish communities for centuries. Enraged citizens went on a rampage, killing nearly fifty Jews, wounding hundreds, and looting and destroying as many as seven hundred homes. For three days neither the police nor the military intervened to stop the violence, leaving the inevitable impression that the pogrom had been either instigated or tolerated by the regime.

The Kishinev pogrom provoked deeply contradictory reactions. For the minster of the interior, Vyacheslav von Plehve, the pogrom was nothing less than a vivid warning to the empire's Jews to remove themselves from the revolutionary cause. When Plehve granted an audience to a group of Jews from Odessa later that spring, he ignored their pleas for assistance and instead berated them in a threatening tone:

> Tell the Jewish youth, your sons and daughters, tell your entire intelligentsia, they should not think that Russia is an old, decaying, and disintegrating body; young and developing Russia will overcome the revolutionary movement. The fear of the Jews is much talked about, but this is not true. The Jews are the most courageous of people. In Western Russia some 90 percent of the revolutionaries are Jews, and in Russia generally—some 40 percent. I shall not conceal from you that the revolutionary movement in Russia worries us . . . but you should know that if you do not deter your youth from the revolutionary movement, we shall make your position untenable to such an extent that you will have to leave Russia, to the very last man!

Later that summer, Theodor Herzl, a prominent Viennese journalist and the founder of modern Zionism, visited Saint Petersburg, where both Plehve and Witte received him. They admitted that tsarist policies were compelling Jews to press for revolution. "If I were a Jew, I too would probably be an enemy of the government," Plehve assured Herzl. For Herzl, the Zionist movement could provide a more hopeful avenue for Jewish resistance, and would end "the defection to the Socialists."

The Jewish Social Democrats around Lenin rejected Herzl's vision and despised the pleadings of self-appointed leaders of Russian Jewry who regarded Jewish resistance to the tsar as an act of self-destruction. Martov denounced any call on the part of Zionists or others for Jews to avoid involvement in Russia's politics. For Martov, this was "detestable reactionary Zionist propaganda," nothing short of an attempt to exploit the devastating impact of the pogroms on the unrefined Jewish masses, as if indifference to politics would protect them. Martov would have none of this logic. It was a nasty formula, "an alliance with autocracy, an alliance with the assassins of Kishinev." For Martov and Lenin, Zionism and any particularist claims on the part of Jews could only play into the hands of reactionary tsarist officials.

Trotsky adopted a similar attitude. No less a figure than Chaim Weizmann, who later became the first president of Israel, came across Plekhanov, Lenin, and Trotsky among groups of Russian Jewish students in Switzerland. These young Jews, who were compelled to study in Switzerland because of restrictions on their education back home, remained anxious over conditions for Jews in Russia. Weizmann was organizing support for the Zionist cause among them. But these Marxist leaders did not hesitate to express their contempt for Jewish national feelings. According to Weizmann, "*They* could not understand why a Russian Jew should want to be anything but a Russian. *They* stamped as unworthy, as intellectually backward, as chauvinist and unmoral, the desire of any Jew to occupy himself with the sufferings and destiny of Jewry."

Trotsky took this a step further. He followed debates at the Sixth Zionist Congress in Basel in the summer of 1903; it was at this meeting that the delegates argued over the British offer of territory in East Africa (the so-called Uganda Project, although the territory involved is in present-day Kenya) for a temporary Jewish homeland, a proposal that Herzl himself had initially accepted before giving in to the pressure of the delegates. Trotsky soon wrote a scathing dismissal of Herzl. Writing in *Iskra* in January 1904, Trotsky dismissed Herzl as "a repulsive figure" and "a shameless adventurist" who was wasting his time soliciting "the aid of the princes of the world." For Trotsky, Zionism was a "tragic mirage." It mattered to him only that Russian Zionists join the Social Democrats and not turn to the Bund once their dreams of a national home in Palestine came to naught. Plekhanov, too, dismissed the Bund as "Zionists who are afraid of seasickness."

But Trotsky was not indifferent to Jewish suffering. He was in London at the time of the Kishinev pogrom, immersed in the work of Lenin's Social Democratic Party. The pogrom affected him deeply, and there are many references to it in his writings and speeches. That spring he became involved in a dispute in Kiev between the Social Democrats and their rivals in the Socialist Revolutionary Party. The Social Democrats were planning to hold a demonstration on May Day just weeks after the violence in Kishinev. But they understood that such a demonstration could turn into a pretext for yet another pogrom, thereby allowing the regime to camouflage its policies by blaming the leftists for its own anti-Jewish measures. Writing in *Iskra* in June, Trotsky weighed in on the side of the Social Democrats:

> Under the acute impression of the Kishinev events, and under the deluge of monstrous rumors spread by the police, Kiev expected pogroms to coincide with the demonstrations. The authorities were preparing to handle the demonstrations brutally under the pretext of quelling a pogrom against the Jews. All had been done in preparation for such a pogrom. Under such conditions, to go out to the streets would have meant to give battle against the enemy in accordance with special conditions created by the enemy. To avoid such a battle did not mean to admit defeat. It meant leaving to oneself the right to choose a more favorable moment.

As the summer approached, Trotsky worked closely with Lenin to plan the Second Congress of the Social Democrats. With *Iskra* as the nucleus for his political party, Lenin was counting on this meeting to consolidate his vision of where the movement could lead. Though he had been in London only nine months, Trotsky was already a compelling figure. His talents as a writer and a speaker figured prominently at the Congress and its aftermath.

The Second Congress of the Social Democrats is now seen as one of the turning points in the history of the Russian revolutionary movement. It opened in Brussels on July 17. But the Belgian police made things so uncomfortable for the delegates that they quickly decamped for England and resumed deliberations in a north London church on July 29. The Congress consisted of forty-four delegates with voting rights and fourteen with consultative status. Trotsky represented the Siberian Social Democratic Workers' Union.

The Congress soon confronted several controversies. The first serious debate concerned the place of the Bund in the Social Democratic movement. The Bund was an avowedly Marxist party. It organized Jewish workers to support a socialist revolution that would recognize the cultural autonomy of the Jews within their communities in Poland and the Russian Empire. It advocated the rights of Jews to preserve Yiddish as their language and, with the hoped-for revolution, to become free and equal citizens within democratic and socialist societies.

The Bund's success and its opposition to assimilation vexed both Jewish and non-Jewish leaders among the Social Democrats. Lenin, in particular, became an outspoken opponent of the Bund. He had his own idea of how to solve the "Jewish Question." He was an advocate of assimilation within the context of a socialist revolution and opposed any support for cultural or national autonomy because it would deflect energy from the primary goal of overthrowing the tsar. At the same time, Lenin was unnerved by the Bund's successful organizing of Jewish workers. The Bund had attracted the allegiance of tens of thousands, particularly in Poland and the western provinces of the Russian Empire, thereby undercutting support for Lenin's Social Democratic underground. Lenin felt that he had to launch attacks against the Bund in *Iskra*. As he asserted in the months before the Second Congress, "Only a Jewish reactionary middle class strongly interested in turning back the wheel of history can rail against 'assimilation activities.'" For Lenin, the fact that the Jews did not inhabit a particular territory of their own and that many were relinquishing "Yiddish for the language of the people among whom they lived" signaled a willingness to abandon their separate identity. Emancipation meant assimilation and salvation for the Jews—literally.

In 1903 the Bund came to the Second Congress insisting that it alone be allowed to represent Jewish workers. Its leaders naively assumed that the Congress would explore how best the *Iskra* group and the Bund could work together with a shared respect for the Bund's unique role among the Jewish masses. But Lenin had something else in mind. He knew that the Bund's approach could only undermine the idea of a centralized, disciplined party of professional revolutionaries. If the Jews were allowed a faction of their own, then the party might collapse into an association of parallel or even competing groups, identified by their ethnic or national origins.

The Second Congress was meeting soon after the Kishinev pogrom in an atmosphere of profound anguish, an atmosphere complicated by the fact that as many as twenty-five of the participants were Jews themselves. Lenin and the *Iskra* group understood that it would be better to have Jewish comrades like Martov and Trotsky speak against the Bund's demands. Trotsky was particularly outspoken, taking the floor many times to answer the Bund and its arguments. Identifying himself and others as members of the Jewish proletariat*—a strategic move designed to make his arguments more credible—Trotsky defended the integrity of the party's program and asserted that if the Bund had its way it would undermine the effectiveness of a united, centralized party. "Do we want to physically destroy those comrades who belong to the Bundist organization?" Trotsky asked rhetorically.

> Do we want to destroy [its] fruitful work in developing the consciousness of the Jewish proletariat? Or is what we want to destroy in the Bund only its special situation in the party? The Bund as the sole representative of the interests of the Jewish proletariat in the party and before the party—or the Bund as the special organization of the party for agitation among the Jewish proletariat? That is how the question must be put. The statute proposed to us has as its goal . . . to raise a wall between us and the Bund. . . . Against that wall the Congress must come out in total unanimity.

For Trotsky, the Bund's insistence that it alone should have the right to organize among Jewish workers implied an underlying suspicion of the non-Jewish members of the party, as if their avowed hatred of antisemitism could not be trusted. "The Bund," Trotsky declared, "is free not to trust the party, but it cannot expect the party to vote no confidence in its own self." Furthermore, if the Bund were allowed to make such a separatist claim within the party, how much more so would it insist on a separate status for the Jews within the nations in which Jews resided?

Speaking as an assimilationist, Trotsky made clear that he foresaw no future for the Jews outside of the communities in which they were living. If it was religion that held Jews together, then the triumph of socialism would lead to the disap-

*The Bund leader Mark Liber immediately challenged Trotsky with a sarcastic aside: "Among whom they have never worked."

pearance of such ties. And if it was an artificial nationalism, as represented either by Zionism or by the Bund, then Trotsky could only denounce both tendencies. His arguments angered the Bund delegates; in their eyes, the *Iskra* editors seemed more determined to oppose Jewish national feeling than to fight antisemitism even after the terrible violence in Kishinev. One Bundist leader denounced Trotsky's "coarse tactlessness." But Trotsky was not deterred. He supported the creation of a disciplined party that would not tolerate factions based on race or nationality. For Trotsky, it was always better to support a universal claim over a parochial concern. Once socialism triumphed, age-old, foolish prejudices would inevitably disappear as an atmosphere of equality and shared prosperity took hold. The Bund's position was overwhelmingly rejected.

Trotsky was equally outspoken over a second controversy. The Social Democrats had long been challenged by other, more conciliatory socialists who adopted what was called a policy of Economism. This approach called for taking up the workers' narrow, economic concerns and not challenging the power of the state. Here, too, Trotsky defended Lenin's approach. The ruling class would accept reforms and concessions to the workers only if it were confronted by revolutionary demands. His speeches were so vehement and so representative of Lenin's thinking that he earned the epithet "Lenin's cudgel." But while the *Iskra* group sided with Lenin, a fundamental disagreement began to emerge that would prove fateful for both the party and for Trotsky.

Lenin felt the board of *Iskra* needed reform. Three of its six editors—Axelrod, Zasulich, and Potresov—were not contributing substantially to the work of the newspaper; it was their general work for the party that was valuable. By dropping them and leaving himself, Plekhanov and Martov, Lenin hoped to make the newspaper more efficient and consolidate his control. But his proposal provoked a host of bad feelings because many of the delegates had deep respect for these honorary editors. Trotsky was among those who were uncomfortable with Lenin's maneuver.

This discussion was quickly followed by what appeared to be a routine debate over who could be considered a member of the party. Two proposals, one by Lenin and a second by Martov, seemed to be roughly equivalent. Lenin's idea limited party membership to activists who "personally participate in one of the party's organizations"; Martov had in mind a more loosely organized party, which would permit individuals to join who "cooperate personally" in party activities but were not necessarily members of a party unit. Like Lenin, Martov recognized the need to organize a party of disciplined, professional conspirators, but he also wanted to create a mass party of workers. This was a circle that could not be squared.

Debates such as these led the party to the fateful split into Bolshevik and Menshevik wings. Under Lenin, the Bolsheviks, as they soon came to be called (the word carries the meaning of "being in the majority," which was, in fact, not altogether true within Russian Social Democracy), adopted more hard-line policies, generally refusing to work with liberal allies and pressing for a dictatorship of the proletariat in place of any possible bourgeois democracy. The Mensheviks ("being in the minority") came to adopt more conciliatory policies, were willing to work with liberal parties to oppose the autocracy, and sustained far greater respect for democratic procedures and civil liberties.

It was here that Trotsky, after weeks of helping to secure victories for Lenin, began to distance himself from Lenin's way of seeing things. What had initially attracted him now troubled him. Although Trotsky remained committed to the creation of a professional party, he also began to interpret Lenin's actions in a different light. He believed that Lenin was adding extraneous requirements for party membership which would hinder the participation of actual workers. Lenin, Trotsky feared, was taking the idea of a centralized party to such an extreme that it would undercut its usefulness and appeal. He could agree with Lenin when it came to the Bund or the unhelpful reform-minded views of the Economists. But as Lenin and Martov found themselves disagreeing over what it meant to be a member of the party, Trotsky turned more toward Martov and away from Lenin. His disillusionment may have been gradual, the result of numerous small disagreements over tone. But Trotsky's break with Lenin, coming in the midst of the Congress, after weeks of having helped to consolidate Lenin's idea of what the party should look like, recalled similarly abrupt changes in his attitude.

Trotsky suddenly became an outspoken, even vituperative, critic. As in his earlier shift to Marxism after opposing it, Trotsky tended to adopt positions that he had once rejected, a personality trait that at times marked his life as a revolutionary. In a report made after the Congress, he denounced Lenin as "the party's disorganizer," a man willing to impose a "state of siege" with "an iron fist." He compared Lenin to Robespierre, except that Lenin was a parody of Robespierre as "a vulgar farce resembles historic tragedy." Their break lasted for fourteen years and was often highlighted by severe polemics in which Trotsky, in particular, denounced Lenin in the most forthright terms.

The Congress left the Social Democrats in disarray; for Trotsky the split in the party was "nothing short of sacrilegious." At the same time, Russia was enduring political upheaval and violence that could only mean more trouble for the autocracy. Poor harvests had left the peasants disgruntled, while the growing class of urban workers openly chafed at lacking recognized unions to represent their interests. The regime dismissed reports of unrest. As Plehve commented, "My police are adequate to the situation." London's *Daily Mail* reported that Plehve dismissed "the energy and courage of the revolutionary organization in Russia, which he thought contented itself with spreading literature and did not dare to resort to violence."

Plehve paid for his complacency. In July 1904 Socialist Revolutionaries assassinated him in Saint Petersburg. Newspapers throughout Europe prominently covered the incident. In Brussels, *L'Indépendance Belge* could not help reminding its readers who the victim was: "The malicious genius of the Russian Empire, . . . Mr. de Plehve was the inspirer of a politics of intransigent reaction. . . . We remember his attitude toward the massacre of the Jews in Kishinev and the scandalous process which followed." Throughout Europe, public opinion deplored the crime without mourning the victim.

As Trotsky followed political developments in Russia, he wrote articles and pamphlets that commanded the attention of other revolutionaries. In August, he published *Our Political Tasks*, a pamphlet dissecting Lenin's approach to power with an intuitive grasp of where it would lead. In just over a hundred tightly argued pages, Trotsky assailed Lenin both personally and politically, dismissing him with unprecedented invective: Lenin was "hideous," "a slovenly attorney," "a malicious and morally repulsive" individual.

Trotsky still shared Lenin's belief in a centralized party of revolutionary conspirators, but now he saw the arrogance at the heart of Lenin's idea. Lenin did not trust the working class. The movement was dominated by a coldhearted intellectual who believed his "orthodox theocracy" could "substitute" itself for the workers, taking them where they needed to go whether or not they agreed with the party's intentions. Trotsky offered a prescient nightmare that would engulf the country they were trying to redeem. "Lenin's methods lead to this," he concluded: "The party organization at first substitutes itself for the party as a whole; then the Central Committee substitutes itself for the organization; and finally a single 'dictator' substitutes himself for the Central Committee." It was only 1904, but Trotsky discerned how the Bolshevik theory of revolution could inevitably lead to a personal dictatorship. Isaac Deutscher observed that "this was the most strident bill of impeachment that any Socialist had ever drawn up against Lenin." It was hard to see how the two men could overcome such a divide.

Trotsky's critique of Lenin and the Bolsheviks underscored his status as an independent Marxist. He inhabited a middle ground between the Bolsheviks and the Mensheviks, leaving him open to either side and giving him freedom to form his own ideas and to react to events as they unfolded without needing to defer to party discipline or to a single-minded leader like Lenin. The events of 1905 made this plain.

The previous year, Japan and Russia had gone to war over their competing interests in the Pacific. Japan was a smaller empire, and Russia was expected to prevail. But the Russian army and navy were not up to the task. The disastrous climax at Port Arthur in January 1905, when the Russian fleet was sunk, marked Russia's humiliating defeat. Lenin had called for support of Japan, arguing that revolutionaries needed to welcome any force that could undermine the authority of the Romanovs. (A decade later he again invoked a defeatist call at the outbreak of World War I.) The war with Japan had dramatically weakened respect for the monarchy. Even so, Lenin was not prepared for the drama soon to unfold in Saint Petersburg. Trotsky was.

On Sunday, January 9, 1905, a peaceful procession of men, women, and children, led by an Orthodox priest named Father Georgy Gapon, made its way to the Winter Palace. They were carrying a petition for Tsar Nicholas II, asking for universal civil rights and a measure of democratic representation. Some carried portraits of the tsar, icons, and church banners to demonstrate their loyalty. The tsar, though, was not in the palace. As the procession approached, the marchers were ordered to disperse. They refused and continued to move forward. The troops stationed in front of the palace grew tense; their commanding officers, unnerved by the size of the crowd and without orders on how to proceed, decided to open fire. Scores of people were killed. History recalls that day as Bloody Sunday. Immediately, strikes broke out all over Russia, accompanied by angry demonstrations and calls for the end to the monarchy.

Trotsky was in Geneva when he heard the news. Exhilarated at the prospect of revolution, he could hardly contain his excitement. "Yes, she has come," he wrote.

> We have awaited her. We have never doubted her. For many years she was only a deduction from our "doctrine," at which the nonentities of every political shade mocked. . . . With her first sweep, she has already uplifted society. . . . Before January 9, our demand for a republic seemed fantastic, doctrinaire, and disgusting to all liberal pundits. One day of revolution was enough, one magnificent contact between the tsar and the people was enough for the idea of constitutional monarchy to become fantastic, doctrinaire, and disgusting. . . . The real monarch has destroyed the idea of the monarch. . . . The revolution has come and she has put an end to our political childhood.

Trotsky could not stay away from Russia, even though he was a fugitive from Siberian exile and faced an immediate sentence of hard labor if caught. He went to Vienna, where he stayed with Victor Adler. Adler "was completely engrossed in Russian affairs, and was obtaining money, passports, addresses" for political émigrés like Trotsky who were streaming back to Russia. Adler arranged for a barber to shave Trotsky's beard and to cut his hair differently, since his "appearance had already become too familiar to the Russian police-agents abroad." Natalia Sedova returned ahead of him to find a suitable and discreet apartment in Kiev; with access to reliable print shops, Kiev was the center of clandestine activity for the Marxist underground. Trotsky joined her there in February, traveling on a false passport. He had been outside of Russia for two and a half years. When he had fled, he was a little-known activist with a flair for writing and organizing. He was now a recognized figure, confident of his theoretical understanding and his authority before a crowd. He would call on all these qualities in the wake of Russia's first revolution.

Trotsky stayed in Kiev for several weeks, living in a series of apartments, at times unnerving his hosts with his frenetic activity. Surrounded by visitors and piles of newspapers, he sent off letters, essays, and proclamations to editors inside and outside of the country. His proclamations circulated widely. While Lenin and Martov stayed outside the country, absorbed in sectarian arguments between Bolsheviks and Mensheviks, Trotsky forged ahead on his own. The situation inside Russia was fluid. The initial wave of strikes and demonstrations ran its course, dampened by arrests and executions. Then, in June, a mutiny by sailors on the battleship *Potemkin* shook the armed forces. The *Potemkin* was the most powerful warship in the Black Sea fleet. Once the sailors took control by shooting or imprisoning the officers, crews on other ships refused to intervene. But the *Potemkin* crew could not sustain its control and eventually surrendered the vessel to Romanian officials. (The incident resonated for years and was immortalized in Sergei Eisenstein's famous film.)

Trotsky reached Saint Petersburg in the spring. He continued to write, while Sedova was arrested "during a cavalry raid on a May Day meeting in the woods," as Trotsky once recalled. She was in jail for about six months and then sent to Tver to live under police supervision. Trotsky was not safe either. Feeling pressure from the secret police, he left Saint Petersburg for Finland later that summer.

As the unrest continued, the tsar was compelled to offer a compromise, a consultative assembly referred to as the Bulygin Duma in honor of the tsar's minister, Alexander Bulygin, who drafted the proposal. It would not be elected based on universal suffrage and would not have the power to enact laws. In his memoirs, Count Witte called the proposed Duma a "monstrosity. . . . It would be a body that would permit those in power to say, in effect: 'We will always listen to what you have to say, but then we will do as we please.'" For Witte, "a parliament with no more than consultative power is the invention of bureaucratic eunuchs."

The government's proposal confused the opposition. The historian Pavel Milyukov, leader of the liberals, accepted the new Duma and urged his followers to vote in the forthcoming elections. The liberals, who coalesced around the party of Constitutional Democrats (known as the Kadets), saw the Duma as the first step toward a constitutional monarchy, akin to the British model of government. Martov and the Mensheviks initially accepted the Duma as well. Lenin and Trotsky both urged a boycott.

Trotsky was scathing in his critique, directing his sarcasm at Milyukov and the liberals. He understood that Tsar Nicholas II had no intention to institute genuine reform; he dismissed halfhearted gestures by the tsar and well-meaning compromises by the liberals. Trotsky denounced Milyukov for declaring that the Bulygin Duma signified the crossing of the Rubicon into constitutional government. "Such things, Professor," he wrote, "are never achieved with the signing of a parchment; they take place on the street and are achieved through struggle. . . . You are afraid of breaking with the Duma, because to you this constitutional mirage seems real in the dry and barren desert through which Russian liberalism has been wading." The liberals were looking to reform the system; Trotsky was looking to overthrow it. In his eyes, no evolutionary process of change could provide sufficient social justice to satisfy his utopian dream.

In August a decree permitted students freedom of assembly on their campuses. Although the government expected this measure to calm hotheaded young people, it had the opposite effect, permitting revolutionary parties to hold rallies and further inflame their passions. The failed war with Japan, which concluded with the Treaty of Portsmouth on September 5— Count Witte represented Russia at a peace conference in New Hampshire led by President Theodore Roosevelt—led to profound disillusionment with the tsar. As Trotsky observed in February 1940, as a larger war in Europe was unfolding: "War does not begin with revolution, but ends with it."

Witte returned to Russia that September. He was appalled by what he found. Baltic provinces were under martial law. Districts in the Caucasus were in open rebellion. Jews in Odessa, where they were in the majority, "decided to use revolutionary means to get rid of their disabilities." Peasants were angry because they still could not own land. Soldiers were restless because they were being blamed "for our disgraceful defeats." As Witte observed, "Revolution was beginning to break out into the open, with a government unable to act, crumbling in some places, and losing authority. . . . In short, the cry was for the end of the regime." The situation reached a crisis in October, when a printers' strike spread throughout the country and quickly involved railway men and workers in other industries.

Still in Finland, Trotsky followed events by reading newspapers from Saint Petersburg. "I opened them one after another," he recalled in *My Life*. "It was like a raging storm coming in through an open window. . . . The revolution was in full swing." He paid his hotel bill and by evening of the same day was "making a speech in the great hall of the Polytechnic Institute in Saint Petersburg." The name of Trotsky would no longer be known only to readers of clandestine pamphlets and proclamations. He was stepping onto the stage of history.

Lenin remained outside the country, fearful for his safety and unclear about how to proceed. He was biding his time. Trotsky had no such qualms. When he returned to Saint Petersburg, he saw a country seething with defiance. The general strike had paralyzed Russia, and the workers, inspired by the idea of electing their own representative body—which became known as the Soviet or council of workers' deputies—wanted more than improved working conditions. They wanted full-scale political reform.

The Soviet was a genuinely democratic institution. Its hundreds of deputies represented around 200,000 workers, about half of the workforce in Saint Petersburg. Both the Mensheviks and the Socialist Revolutionaries dispatched their representatives and supported the work of the Soviet. Trotsky, in fact, first appeared at the Soviet as a representative of the Mensheviks. The Bolsheviks were also represented but had the arrogance to urge the Soviet to yield to their leadership; that idea went nowhere.

Faced by the strike and a determined working class, the tsar backed down and issued the famous Constitutional Manifesto on October 17. It had been written by Witte. The Manifesto overturned political life. According to the Manifesto, Russia would soon have a genuine parliament, while the government pledged to honor personal freedom, civil liberties, and universal suffrage. If the tsar and his ministers expected that this concession would calm things down, they were soon cured of their naivete. The Soviet quickly recognized Trotsky's authority and made him vice chairman. Although the chairman was a young, little-known attorney named Grigory Khrustalev-Nosar, Trotsky was the moving force behind the Soviet's appeal. He wrote the manifestoes, edited its bulletin, and was the most recognized orator in the city. At one point, he was editing and writing for three newspapers.

Lenin, by contrast, was stuck in Europe and had yet to address a real crowd. The Bolsheviks in the capital (and Lenin in Europe) remained wary of the Soviet, fearing that "an elected nonparty organization [would offer] competition with the party." Trotsky saw things differently. For him, the Soviet could be more than a vehicle to promote the rights of the workers or issue calls for dramatic reform; it could be turned into a shadow government, an alternative to the autocracy itself, at least in the capital.

Led by Trotsky, the Soviet also recognized the need to defend the Jews from pogroms. In response to the wave of strikes, the government had encouraged pogroms throughout the Pale of Settlement, led by the Black Hundreds, an extreme reactionary movement that emerged at the outset of the twentieth century to support the tsar and to carry out violent propaganda and murderous attacks on revolutionaries and Jews. What better way to divert the energy and anger of the population? The scale of the violence was unprecedented. In less than two weeks, immediately following the October Manifesto, pogroms broke out in nearly seven hundred communities. In one day in Odessa, eight hundred Jews were murdered. Extending into September 1906, the attacks claimed more than three thousand Jewish lives.

For Trotsky, the tsar was "a tireless hangman." Nicholas II, in fact, believed that "nine-tenths of the troublemakers are Jews," as he wrote to his mother that fall. In October the Soviet learned of plans to stage a pogrom in the capital itself to coincide with a funeral in honor of the Soviet's fallen martyrs. Trotsky sensed the Soviet's vulnerability—and the likelihood of terrible violence—and urged his colleagues to cancel the funeral. They reluctantly accepted. At the same time, determined not to back down altogether, they organized armed units to defend Jews living in Saint Petersburg. According to one source, as many as twelve thousand men, armed with revolvers, or with wooden or metal clubs, were mobilized to fight the Black Hundreds if they attempted a pogrom: this move effectively forestalled the regime's attacks.*

*In his account of the 1905 revolution, Trotsky wrote about the social and political factors that stirred up the pogroms.

The general strike was now over, but inspired by Trotsky, the Soviet issued new demands: that the government declare an amnesty for political prisoners, remove army detachments from Saint Petersburg, allow the creation of a people's militia, and recognize an eight-hour workday. Again, the tsar backed down, granting a political amnesty with the hope that yet another concession would guarantee his authority. Only then did Lenin feel safe returning to Russia.

Back in the capital in November, Lenin understood that the Bolsheviks had to accept the Soviet and find a way to work with it. And when he saw Trotsky's dynamic leadership, Lenin was man enough to concede his preeminence. "Trotsky has won this by his tireless and striking work," he said to a colleague. With the granting of personal freedom, revolutionaries like Trotsky were speaking before huge crowds, while the police, obliged to honor the tsar's promise, stood helplessly by. The opposition press flourished. As leader of the Saint Petersburg Soviet, Trotsky led the takeover of a small newspaper, *Russkaya Gazeta* (Russian gazette). "Within a few days," he recalled, "the circulation rose from thirty thousand to one hundred thousand. A month later, it had reached the half-million mark." Both the Bolshevik *Novaya Zhizn* (New life) and the Menshevik *Nachalo* (Beginning) enjoyed circulations of more than fifty thousand, their publication supported by wealthy businessmen who accepted the stark reality that Russia could no longer live as before.

The Soviet challenged the tsar and appeared to threaten his throne. (Max Eastman, who for a time promoted Trotsky's image in the West, wrote about 1905 that Trotsky "actually wielded for some days an authority in Russia exceeding that of the Tsar." This was a gross exaggeration.) The Soviet remained in place for fifty-two days. Count Witte, now serving as the tsar's prime minister, patiently waited for the workers and their allies to lose their resolve. He began to reimpose censorship.

Calls for another general strike drew little response. Army units stopped paying attention to revolutionary appeals. On December 3 Witte ordered troops to surround the Soviet. Trotsky, in an act of political and moral clarity, shouted to his followers not to resist but to dismantle their revolvers rather than surrender them. He and other leaders were taken into custody.

But the revolution was not yet over. The Moscow Soviet, which had been established in October, remained determined to resist. Joined by high school and university students, rebellious workers constructed barricades in the streets. Their defiance lasted for ten days before the tsar dispatched loyal army units. Equipped with heavy weapons, they killed more than a thousand people, including prisoners and unarmed civilians.

Trotsky looked back on the 1905 revolution as a "dress rehearsal," full of grim lessons that would serve him well in 1917. In his eyes, "It was not the opposition of the liberal bourgeoisie, not the elemental risings of the peasantry or the terrorist acts of the intelligentsia, but the strike of the workers that for the first time brought tsarism to its knees." His theoretical claims and intuitions as a Marxist were confirmed. It would be the proletariat that would have to seize power; it would be the workers who would take over the destiny of Russia.

Trotsky was held for about ten months in pretrial detention with other leaders of the Soviet in the famous prisons of Saint Petersburg, first in Kresty, then in the Peter and Paul Fortress along the banks of the Neva River. He and his comrades were treated with a good deal of deference. Their cell doors were not locked, and they were permitted to read books delivered from outside the prison, to meet with each other, even to discuss the political challenges that lay ahead. During these months his first son, Lev, was born.

Trotsky quickly established an industrious routine. Fluent in German and French, he spent hours a day reading serious literature. He luxuriated in his free time. "As I lay in my prison bunk I absorbed [the European classics] with the same sense of physical delight that the gourmet has in sipping choice wines or in inhaling the fragrant smoke of a fine cigar." He also wrote a good deal. One work, in particular, reverberated for the rest of his life.

Among Bolsheviks and Mensheviks—who actually drew closer together in 1905 in response to the turmoil in Russia—there was a consensus that revolutions had to follow a particular pattern. Feudal societies would experience industrialization, giving rise to an urban middle class. This class would take power—the so-called bourgeois revolution—instituting parliamentary democracy, which would include free elections and civil liberties. But the inevitable exploitation of the urban proletariat would make capitalism vulnerable to revolution. In line with this understanding of Marx, a country like Germany, blessed with a large and politically astute working class, would be the first to see a proletarian revolution. (In Marxist terms, Germany's working class was more mature, more highly developed than others.) But Russian Marxists faced a perplexing dilemma. Capitalism was relatively undeveloped in Russia, and the country had yet to experience a bourgeois revolution. The tsar remained on his throne, exercising unquestioned authority, while the Russian middle class was weak and indecisive. It was the workers, in Trotsky's eyes, who had nearly toppled the tsar in 1905. But their revolutionary initiative undercut classical Marxist tenets.

Trotsky wanted to make sense of how a Marxist revolution could develop in a backward society. Pondering this dilemma, he devised two famous theories: of uneven and combined development, and of permanent revolution. In fact, he had initially developed these ideas in 1904, when he found himself spending time in Zurich with another revolutionary named Alexander Helphand, or Parvus, his party pseudonym. But it was in 1906, when Trotsky was reading and writing all day in a

Saint Petersburg prison, that he systematically formulated his theories in a collection of essays entitled *The Balance and the Prospects: The Moving Forces of the Revolution.* According to Trotsky, only a superficial reading of Marx required one to believe that a proletarian revolution could succeed solely in a country with a highly developed capitalist system and a strong middle class, like Germany. Trotsky argued that Russia's relative backwardness, particularly its lack of a middle class and its lack of capital, could enhance the prospects for revolution, make revolution even more likely if not inevitable. Russia was already creating an urban proletariat without developing a full-fledged capitalist system. If the proletariat gained power in Russia, it could complete the process of modernization normally reserved for the bourgeoisie, a process of capitalist development that had characterized the countries of Western Europe. In this sense, Trotsky was trying to analyze the prospects for revolution in Russia within a set of Marxist categories—as he understood them—rather than trying to apply Marxist principles in some kind of mechanical way.

In Russia the revolution could occur simultaneously within both the bourgeoisie and the proletariat, in effect skipping over the bourgeois phase. The workers would take power themselves, then declare a dictatorship of the proletariat. With power consolidated in their hands, this new government, by and for the benefit of the workers, would initially be isolated and face the wrath of capitalist countries. Trotsky's idea of permanent revolution meant that socialism could not succeed in one country, particularly a country like Russia whose economic development lagged so completely behind other, more advanced countries. To sustain power, the government of Russian workers would have to inspire revolutions in more economically developed European countries, which would then come to its assistance. The theory of permanent revolution lent Trotsky's name a particular allure. It provoked endless debate and controversy within Social Democratic circles and helped separate him from Lenin.

But sitting in jail, Trotsky had more to do than explore European literature and develop a new theory of revolution. All the defendants needed to prepare for their appearance before a tsarist court. Mensheviks leaders who remained at liberty, led by Yuli Martov, wanted them to defend themselves within the framework of the October Manifesto: the tsar had guaranteed civil liberties, and their actions as leaders of the Soviet did not violate either the letter or the spirit of the Manifesto. It was the tsar who had violated the law by arresting them. But Trotsky could not accept Martov's approach: It would deny that the Soviet had been willing to seize power through an armed insurrection and would lend legitimacy to tsarist rule. Trotsky was not interested in defending himself in the ordinary sense. He intended to appeal to a higher authority—the revolutionary masses. He wanted to put the regime on trial. Lenin and the Bolsheviks supported his intention to confront the court. His longtime comrade Grigory Ziv, who was also in prison in Saint Petersburg, later recalled that Trotsky was "full of warm sympathy for the Bolsheviks to whom he was spiritually akin, and of a hardly suppressed antipathy to the Mensheviks." In prison together, the defendants worked out a shared legal strategy, assigning Trotsky the task of explaining their political preparations for an armed uprising.

The trial began on September 19, 1906. Charged with planning an armed insurrection, the defendants faced a civilian court rather than a military tribunal. The difference was not trivial; under Russian law, they could not face the death penalty. Trotsky's parents were in the courtroom. Anxious for her son's future, his mother seemed confused by the proceedings. His father, more appreciative of Trotsky's stature and eloquence, sat "pale, silent, happy, and distressed, all in one," as Trotsky himself recalled.

The trial did not unfold as the regime intended. Mindful of the defendants' popularity in the capital, the government "turned the court building and the adjoining streets . . . into a military camp." But the public was not intimidated and flooded the courtroom with flowers and other gifts for the defendants. There were forty attorneys on the defense team. More than two hundred witnesses offered evidence, Trotsky wrote, among them "workers, manufacturers, members of the secret police, engineers, servants, citizens, journalists, post office officials, police chiefs, gymnasium students, municipal councilors, janitors, senators, hooligans, deputies, professors, soldiers." They were all subjected to cross-examination, especially by the defendants, who had nothing to hide and were eager to detail the work of the Soviet.

Trotsky took the stand on October 4. His testimony was the high point of the trial. Undeterred by the advice of his defense counsel, Trotsky spoke explicitly about two of the most volatile issues on everyone's mind: the question of armed insurrection on the part of the Soviet and the government's use of pogroms. He did not mince words.

Did the Soviet . . . consider itself justified in using force and repressive measures in certain instances? To this question, posed in this general form, my answer is: Yes. . . . In the conditions created by a political general strike, the essence of which was that it paralyzed the mechanism of government, the old governmental force that had long outlived its day and against which the political strike was directed, proved itself completely incapable of undertaking anything. Even with the barbarous means which alone were at its disposal, it was not in a position to maintain and regulate public order. In the meantime the strike had thrown hundreds of thousands of workers from the factories into the street and had awakened them to public political life. Who could take over the direction of those masses, who could carry discipline into their ranks? Which organ of the old governmental power? The police? The gendarmerie? . . . I find only one answer: nobody, except the Council of Workers' Deputies.

Brave and insightful, Trotsky's speech expressed his full belief in revolutionary change. But he was not finished. Next he turned to the pogroms. There are relatively few times in his career when Trotsky publicly spoke of violence against his fellow Jews. He did not regard his Jewish origins as his primary identity, and he dismissed the idea that Jewish suffering was among the reasons for his hatred of the tsarist regime. But he detested pogroms and understood how the Russian government unleashed them, both to punish innocent Jewish families for the revolutionary activity of other Jews and to distract its own followers from the true causes of the country's turmoil. Trotsky never abided physical attacks on Jews, and often intervened to denounce such violence and organize a defense. "We had no doubt that behind the facade of the Black Hundreds was the powerful fist of the ruling clique," he told the court.

> What we possess is not a national governmental force but an automaton for mass murder. I can find no other name for the machine of government that cuts into pieces the living flesh of our people. And if you tell me that the pogroms, the arson, the violence . . . if you tell me that all that has happened in Tver, Rostov, Kursk, Siedlce . . . if you tell me that Kishinev, Odessa, Bialystok represent the form of government of the Russian Empire, then yes, then I recognize, together with the prosecution, that in October and November we were arming ourselves against the form of government of the Russian Empire.

No non-Jewish revolutionary had ever confronted tsarist officials with such defiant words about their violent, antisemitic animosity.

In a delicious irony, the court was soon confronted by incontrovertible evidence of the regime's complicity in the pogroms. A former director of the police in Saint Petersburg wrote two letters to Trotsky's defense attorney offering to testify and to provide material evidence of the government's hand in the pogroms. According to Lopukhin, the tsar's secret police—the Okhrana—had printed leaflets calling for pogroms throughout the empire. Lopukhin also offered to testify that it was only the actions of the Soviet that had averted a pogrom in October 1905, the very attack that Trotsky and his colleagues had successfully prevented. The court refused to permit Lopukhin to testify and barred his evidence from the record; to admit it would have provided a devastating indictment of the regime itself, something the judges could not allow. Faced by this adamant refusal, the defendants left the courtroom and boycotted the remainder of the proceedings. The guilty verdict was delivered before a virtually empty courtroom on November 2. Although the defendants were acquitted of the principal charge of insurrection, they were convicted of numerous other crimes, then sentenced in absentia to Siberian exile for life.

Just two months later, the convoy of prisoners, some accompanied by wives and children, was hurried to the railroad station and put on a train headed eastward. Once across the Urals, they reached Tyumen, where they were transferred to a convoy of forty horse-driven sledges and taken to Tobolsk. Only here were they told their final destination: the penal colony at Obdorsk, a remote location on the Arctic Circle nearly a thousand miles from any railroad station. Trotsky now understood that the farther they traveled, the more difficult escape would become. "Every day we move down one step into the kingdom of cold and wilderness," he wrote in a notebook. He was not sure what to do. He sent instructions to his wife, asking her to send him books and assuring her that, with a thousand residents, Obdorsk would provide a place for them to live together with their infant son.

But his fortunes changed when the convoy reached the small town of Berezov. Able to walk about, Trotsky met another political exile, a doctor, who suggested that he could avoid continuing on the journey northward if he were to simulate sciatica. The police would place him under surveillance in a hospital, but from there, with some luck, he could find a peasant to help him escape. Within days, Trotsky evaded the local police and set off, wrapped in warm furs, in a sleigh drawn by reindeer and driven by an astute but constantly drunken guide. Trotsky came to love and admire the reindeer. "I had the same feeling for these animals that an aviator must have for his motor when he flies over an ocean at an altitude of several hundred feet," he wrote in his memoirs.

It took them a week to cross hundreds of miles of tundra, in the dead of winter, with little to eat. They would boil snow to make water, sit on the snow, and drink tea. Trotsky carried a few bottles of liquor, thinking he could use them to barter for food or other necessities. Finally, they reached a small settlement in the Urals, with a train station from where he was able to reach Perm. From there, he headed to Saint Petersburg and a reunion with his wife and son. Stepping outside on the train platform, where he could feel the wind in his face, Trotsky suddenly experienced a profound sense of liberation, and "a loud cry burst from me spontaneously—a cry of joy and freedom." Once he reached Saint Petersburg, he stayed for only a few days, knowing that the police would soon be on his trail. He and his family left for Finland, where political émigrés had been heading since the collapse of the 1905 revolution. Both Lenin and Martov were in Helsinki to greet him. Lenin, Martov, and Trotsky did not return to Russia until the spring of 1917. By that time, Tsar Nicholas II was no longer on the throne, and Lenin and Trotsky would complete the revolution.

3

An Independent Marxist

ALTHOUGH THE REVOLUTION of 1905 compelled the tsar to make substantial concessions, these reforms were quickly reversed as the autocracy regained control of the country and ruthlessly asserted its revived power. By June 1907 Tsar Nicholas II had dispersed the Second Duma, arrested Bolshevik representatives—both Lenin and Trotsky had shifted their strategies and supported the idea of Social Democrats standing for the Second Duma, thinking it could prove useful for spreading their ideas—and dispatched them to Siberia. The regime also hunted down several thousand would-be revolutionaries and executed them after summary trials.

Trotsky was safe in Europe, hailed as the legendary head of the Saint Petersburg Soviet who had defied the tsar in the streets and in the courtroom. He arrived in London at the end of April 1907 to attend the fifth Party Congress. A host of major figures were there. The writer Maxim Gorky sought out Trotsky and made a point of praising his political pamphlets.

Trotsky discussed revolutionary theory with the German militant Rosa Luxemburg, who shared many of his views. Years later, after her brutal death at the hands of German reactionaries in 1919, he recalled her with genuine tenderness. "She was a little woman, frail, and even sickly looking, but with a noble face, and beautiful eyes that radiated intelligence; she captivated one by the sheer courage of her mind and character."

On the face of things, the party seemed full of dynamic possibilities. Three hundred fifty delegates crowded into a church hall—ten times as many as had attended in London five years earlier. Meeting as a united party for the last time, Bolsheviks and Mensheviks argued over how best to participate in the Second Duma and over the role of the peasants and Russian liberalism in the struggle against the autocracy.

Trotsky also continued his dispute with Lenin. Lenin hoped to bring him back into the fold, and there were moments when their views coincided—for example, Lenin welcomed Trotsky's statement about the need to organize both workers and peasants. But Trotsky continued to keep his own counsel, eager to encourage reconciliation between Bolsheviks and Mensheviks even as he found himself siding more with the Mensheviks than with Lenin.

Like Martov, Trotsky joined in the criticism of the Bolshevik "expropriations," the bank robberies in the Caucasus that many suspected Lenin had supported to secure needed funds for party activities. Joseph Stalin was at the congress, as well.* He listened to the debates but offered no opinion, even though he was heavily involved in the "expropriations"; the Congress insisted that Lenin stop the bank raids. Trotsky did not meet or even notice Stalin, but Stalin took note of Trotsky. Shortly af-

*Djugashvili was to assume the name Stalin in January 1913.

terward, in a report on the congress, he referred to Trotsky's "beautiful uselessness," as though he were little more than an overrated windbag. The reality was that Bolsheviks and Mensheviks alike were facing a period of dispiriting reaction during which they grew farther apart. A decade passed before World War I unlocked the gate to revolution.

With the congress behind him, Trotsky had to find a place for himself and his family, in both the revolutionary movement and European society. He wanted to live in Berlin, where he could observe Europe's strongest Marxist party, the German Social Democrats. But the police made it clear that he was not welcome. By the fall of 1907 he and Sedova and their son, Lev, had settled in Vienna. He relied on his wits and his pen to earn a living. He wrote for socialist newspapers in Europe, and for the Bolshevik *Proletary* (Proletarian) and the Menshevik *Luch* (The ray), which were permitted to circulate in Russia. He also contributed articles to a small newspaper edited by his mother's relative, Moisey Shpentzer, in Odessa. But he earned most of his living as the Vienna correspondent for the liberal *Kievskaya Mysl* (Kievan thought), which had a large, enthusiastic following throughout southern Russia. "I wrote there on the most diverse subjects, sometimes very risky as regards censorship. . . . Of course I couldn't say all that I wanted to in a legally published, nonpartisan paper. But I never wrote what I did not want to say," Trotsky recalled in *My Life*.

Trotsky came to know the cream of European radicalism: August Bebel of Germany, who had once confronted Otto Bismarck, the imposing chancellor of Germany; Jean Jaurès, the famous socialist leader of France; and Karl Kautsky, a revered figure among Marxists in Austria and throughout Europe. Trotsky also worked closely with Adolph Yoffe, a fellow revolutionary, who had been born and raised in Saint Petersburg. Yoffe suffered from nervous breakdowns and sought help from one of Freud's disciplines, Alfred Adler. Adler was among the founders of the psychoanalytic movement and had originated the concept of the inferiority complex. Trotsky came to know Adler as well, and grew intrigued by Freud's theories. Trotsky never lost his fascination with Freud and later did not hesitate to encourage fellow Bolsheviks to study Freud and consider how Marxism and psychoanalysis might have more in common than Marxists in particular would care to recognize.

As the prospects for revolution in Russia waned, Trotsky created a life for himself and his family that was far broader than the cramped, inward-looking existence of his fellow revolutionaries. He read widely in European literature, visited museums, and traveled throughout the continent to speak at socialist conferences. He and his wife had a second son, Sergei, in 1908. When the boys grew old enough to enter public elementary school in Vienna, regulations required religious instruction in the faith of their parents. Trotsky had been born a Jew, Sedova Greek Orthodox. Both were militant atheists and would have been happy to ignore the school regulations. But they had little choice and so decided to designate the Lutheran faith, which was common among Jews who chose to convert in Russia and Eastern Europe. As Trotsky wrote, it was "easier on the children's shoulders as well their souls."

Within a year, Trotsky was editing a newspaper of his own. Called *Pravda* (Truth), it had been founded in 1905 by a small Menshevik group in Ukraine. Trotsky took over the newspaper in October 1908. His work with *Pravda* involved more than editing and writing. The newspaper had to be smuggled into Russia, and Trotsky, with the help of assistants, pasted copies into cardboard tubes, then packed art posters inside so they could be safely sent into Russia by mail. He also grew friendly with Russian sailors who helped smuggle copies through the

Black Sea. Strapped for funds, he coaxed support from other socialists to sustain the venture and often relied on his wife's willingness to pawn family valuables. At times, he sold his own books for the extra cash.

Pravda built an audience and engaged readers inside and outside of Russia. Using it as his base, Trotsky tried to unite the two wings of the Social Democratic movement. But neither the Bolsheviks nor the Mensheviks warmed to his position. Lenin would have welcomed unity, but only on his own terms. He was not interested in compromising to reach agreement with the Mensheviks; he wanted their capitulation. He reacted with indifference to Trotsky's attempts at reconciliation. As for the Mensheviks, they knew that Trotsky generally sided with them and so could only wonder why he wanted to promote unity so badly.

Trotsky's continual call for unity had an aspect of naive idealism. He understood the ideological differences between Bolsheviks and Mensheviks. But during a period of tsarist resurgence, Trotsky wanted Bolsheviks and Mensheviks to reinforce each other's effectiveness rather than dissipate their collective energy with useless polemical arguments. His efforts, meanwhile, led nowhere and betrayed an inability to recognize political reality. Staking out his place as an independent Marxist, he set a pattern that years later would help assure his undoing. Proud, determined, happy to go it alone, he did not nurture a following in either wing of the party.

By the spring of 1912, *Pravda* had such luster among Social Democrats that Lenin expropriated its name for a daily newspaper of his own, delegating Joseph Stalin, who was now living in Saint Petersburg, to publish it there. Trotsky protested but eventually gave in. The new *Pravda* secured a place in history, leaving Trotsky's Viennese *Pravda* a forgotten ancestor.

Trotsky enjoyed living in Europe, but he remained alert to undercurrents of tension below everyday life. In October 1912 a conflict broke out in the Balkan Peninsula that led to two nasty wars. At that time, the region was divided among six independent states: Greece, Turkey, Romania, Bulgaria, Serbia, and Montenegro, along with the Austro-Hungarian provinces of Dalmatia, Bosnia, and Herzegovina. The First Balkan War pitted Bulgaria against Turkey. Bulgaria made significant gains before the Treaty of London ended the initial war. Hostilities broke out again in 1913, when Bulgaria attacked Serbia, provoking an alliance of Turkey, Greece, and Romania to declare war on Bulgaria.

Trotsky covered both the First and Second Balkan Wars for *Kievskaya Mysl*. He traveled first to Belgrade and then to Sofia, where he witnessed Bulgaria's declaration of war. He saw refugees crowded into railroad stations, interviewed soldiers back from the front, and came upon obtuse and uninformed European journalists who failed to understand the gravity of the conflict. His description of a British correspondent belongs among the classic portraits from that era:

> He is magnificent, this ambassador of the press. His legs, with their self-confident thick rotundities, take up half the compartment. Wearing thick stockings and leggings above fireproof boots, dressed in a suit of thick gray-checked material, with a short stout pipe of the best quality between his teeth, with a precisely etched parting in his hair, and with two yellow trunks made out of the hide of some prehistoric animal, he sits motionless reading Anatole France. . . . He is visiting the Balkan Peninsula for the first time, knows none of the Slavonic languages, does not speak a word of German, has only such command of French as is compatible with the dignity of a self-respecting Briton, does not look out of the window, and talks to no one. Armed with this panoply of qualities he is going to survey the political destinies of the Balkans.

Trotsky relied on his powers of observation and sharp polemical style to convey the complexity of the tragedy. "The frontiers between the dwarf states of the Balkan Peninsula were drawn not in accordance with national conditions or national demands," he told his readers, "but as a result of wars, diplomatic intrigues, and dynastic interests. The Great Powers—in the first place, Russia and Austria—have always had a direct interest in setting the Balkan peoples and states against each other and then, when they have weakened one another, subjecting them to their economic and political influence." All this had already led to "wars between Greece and Turkey, Turkey and Bulgaria, Romania and Greece, Bulgaria and Serbia." For Trotsky, surveying the sorry history of a region "so kindly favored by nature and so cruelly mutilated by history," the only solution was a Balkan federal republic.

Trotsky discovered a good many things to scorn: censorship in Bulgaria and in Russia, where a section of the press "has replaced newsprint by a calfskin stretched over a drumhead"; Turkish atrocities against Armenians; and a cavalier attitude in Bulgaria toward outbreaks of cholera. At times, Trotsky sounded as if he was succumbing to pacifism as he watched the burning of Albanian villages by Bulgarian forces. "This was the first real, authentic instance I had seen in the theater of war, of ruthless mutual extermination between men." He concluded that "man is dependent on conditions. In the circumstances of the organized brutality of war, men quickly become brutalized without realizing it."

Covering these two wars, Trotsky understood how the conflicts were bequeathing "an extreme intensification of national hatreds." And it was here, as he surveyed impoverished Jews in Sofia and numerous Jewish villages in Romania, that Trotsky produced his most extensive writing about the fate of his coreligionists.

He did not conceal his distaste for poor, religious Jews in Sofia. Under the weight of extreme poverty, they "comfort themselves with the legend of the coming kingdom of Zion," a backhanded dismissal of their Zionist longings. Their huts re-called the degradation of the Jewish villages of his childhood, where traditional Jewish homes could not compare with the clean, well-kept abodes of their German neighbors. For Trot-sky, only socialism pointed the way out of the ghetto, and he left heartened by the presence of Jewish radicals, workers who had "escaped from the spell of religious melodies and national superstitions and transferred their hopes to the socialist inter-national of labor." Nothing gave him greater pleasure than to meet a Jewish trade union organizer with a portrait of Karl Marx on his wall.

In August 1913 Trotsky contributed three substantial arti-cles about Romanian Jews to *Kievskaya Mysl.* Invoking all the anger he could muster, Trotsky made clear that the 300,000 Jews of Romania, deprived of citizenship, were among the most persecuted people in all of Europe. Myriad laws restricted their participation in civic life, where they could live, and how much land they could own. Jewish children were barred from attend-ing state primary schools. "A Jew cannot become a lawyer, the owner of a chemist's shop, a dealer, or a broker on the stock ex-change," he reported. But the government required Jews to pay taxes and drafted them into the army as if they were normal cit-izens. He could only conclude that "Antisemitism has become the state religion, the last psychological cement holding to-gether a feudal society that is rotten through and through."

Trotsky went on to describe the failure of the European Powers to protect the Jews of Romania. Under the Treaty of Berlin of 1878, Romania was obligated to grant equal rights to all of her national minorities. Trotsky expressed astonishment in reporting that German Chancellor Otto von Bismarck had spoken out vigorously in defense of Romania's Jews around that time. "Acting in a sense as the executor of the Congress of Berlin, [Bismarck] refused to enter into any direct diplomatic dealings with Bucharest as long as the Jews had not been granted equal rights. . . . It was remarkable," Trotsky explained, "how close to the Iron Chancellor's heart were the interests of Moldavian Jewry; the interests of the Hohenzollern on that eastern throne were nothing to him beside the fate of some pariahs without rights."

Then Trotsky revealed the deeper story behind Bismarck's apparent sensitivity. The chancellor was engaging in a complex maneuver to pressure the Romanian government to buy shares of the Romanian railroad, which had been generously financed by German bankers, who then went bankrupt as the project foundered. And the Jewish banker Baron Gerson von Bleichröder—who was personally close to Bismarck and Kaiser Wilhelm I—was among the leading financiers looking to recoup his losses. "It gradually became clear that this was Bismarck's *main* condition. The lean abstractions of Jewish equality of rights were eaten up by the fat shares of Bleichröder's banks." Bismarck had his way. "The matter amounted to . . . a colossal piece of financial and political blackmail, in which what was at stake was the 100 million marks invested by the Prussian nobility, . . . [while] the rights of Romania's Jews served as the means of extortion." Once the deal was closed, the "'settlement' of the Jewish Question was reduced to an empty formality with the naturalization of 900 Jews who had served in the Turkish campaign of 1876–78. The remaining 299,100 Jews were left in the same situation as before the Congress of Berlin. . . . When you read the diplomatic documents concerning this affair, and the private correspondence of the parties involved in it, you are never free from a feeling of profound disgust," Trotsky concluded.

But he was not finished. After detailing the plight of Romanian Jewry and the sordid diplomatic maneuvering that exploited it, Trotsky went on to criticize the newly formed Union of Romanian Jews for refusing "to undertake vigorous agitation among the masses, to fraternize with the democratic elements of the Romanian people, to make an open appeal to the public opinion of the working people of Europe." Instead, these Jewish leaders took pride in their "temporizing passivity," hoping to gain credibility with the "enlightened discretion of the ruling oligarchy" by proclaiming their patriotism and fighting alongside Romanian antisemites "for a piece of someone else's land."

These articles have a surprising, almost novel quality. Faced with the reality of Jewish suffering at the hands of a reactionary regime, whose repressive measures bore a striking resemblance to the tsar's, Trotsky called for emancipation and equal rights; he did not revert to calling for class struggle or a proletarian revolution. He almost sounded like an old-fashioned liberal out to promote civil liberties.

While Trotsky was in the Balkans, the case of Mendel Beilis commanded the attention of Russian society. The case had started in March 1911, when a twelve-year-old boy named Andrei Yushchinsky was murdered in Kiev and his body thrown into the Dnieper River. The likely perpetrators were ignored while the police, under instructions from the Ministry of Justice, framed a Jew for the crime. They chose Beilis, a modest worker in a brick factory, and accused him of killing the boy in order to use his blood in the preparation of matzoh for the Passover holiday. Protests erupted throughout the world, including in the liberal and radical press of Russia. In Czechoslovakia, Thomas Masaryk led a demonstration to protest the case, while the United States abrogated its commercial treaty with Russia in part over the blood libel accusation.

But prosecutors refused to relent and proceeded with a trial by jury in September 1913. Trotsky was back in Vienna and able to follow the case in a daily verbatim account in *Kievskaya Mysl*. It is notable that at least three attorneys associated with Beilis's defense had some connection to Trotsky:

Oskar Gruzenberg and A. S. Zarudny had participated in his defense during the case of the Saint Petersburg Soviet in 1906, and Alexander Kerensky later led the Provisional Government after the abdication of Tsar Nicholas II. It was Kerensky's government that Lenin and Trotsky overthrew in the fall of 1917.

Trotsky portrayed the Beilis case as a deliberate attempt by the autocracy to stir up hatred of the Jews. Most of the initiative came from the notorious minister of justice, Ivan Shcheglovitov,* who was behind the indictment, as well as from local officials. Trotsky could not restrain his anger. The following material, from a much longer piece, which appeared in the Viennese newspaper *Die Neue Zeit* (The new times) soon after Beilis was acquitted, captures the full force of Trotsky's sarcastic fury. Once the trial got under way, the prosecution arrayed its considerable tools. As Trotsky described it,

> There is the expertise for ritual, there are the volumes of material evidence, which can stun the jury, and most of all, there is a living Jew with a crooked nose and a black beard. . . . There was nothing startling in the very buildup of the accusation; what was stunning was the deliberate falsity of it. But when an ordinary Jewish worker . . . is suddenly torn away from his wife and children, and is told that he has drained out the blood of a living child, with a view to consuming it, in one form or another, to the joy of his Jehovah, then one need only visualize for a moment the state of this wretch during twenty-six months of isolated imprisonment to cause one's hair to stand on end. . . . Every effort was done to instill hatred toward Beilis as a Jew in the Kievan jury.

During the trial itself, all of Russia seemed to pass through the courtroom:

*Shcheglovitov was killed during a wave of executions by the Bolsheviks in Moscow that followed a failed attempt to assassinate Lenin in August 1918.

A suburban shoemaker, a Jewish capitalist, a peasant dray-
man, a police detective, street arabs, liberal journalists,
thieves, a Greek Orthodox monk (a Jewish convert), a con-
vict, spinsters of light conduct, a priest, an officer of the gendarmerie, a cashier of a bankrupt loan bank in the role of a
leading patriot, a former revolutionary in the role of a voluntary investigator, a lawyer-witness, a medical professor,
a Catholic priest, a professor of a spiritual academy and a
Jewish rabbi—thieves and "reputable" people, learned spe-
cialists and fanatics, refuse of pogromist reaction and revolutionary splinters—all these passed before the amazed eyes
of twelve obscure people, chiefly peasants, deliberately
placed there by the minister of justice for the greatest convenience of the medieval trial court.

Relieved by the jury's unexpected vote to acquit (although it did
declare that a ritual murder had been perpetrated by someone
unknown), Trotsky reviewed the trial transcript and observed
that he had reacted "first and foremost with a feeling of physical nausea."

It is hard to sort out the motivations behind Trotsky's
complex reaction to the Beilis trial or the conditions facing Romanian Jewry. His commitment to social justice had several
sources. Neither he nor people close to him ever asserted that
his moral education was formed by his experience as a young,
sensitive, intellectually precocious Jew in an empire ruled by an
antisemitic autocrat. In his memoirs, Trotsky has little if anything to say about childhood experiences of antisemitism. There
are vivid examples of Russian Jews from families that were at
least somewhat assimilated, who nonetheless recalled the anguish of their parents at news of pogroms or the unfolding
Dreyfus case. If such incidents occurred in Trotsky's childhood
home, he did not share them. But as he came across impoverished and disenfranchised Jews in the Balkans and followed the
notorious Beilis case, he responded with an angry eloquence.

Twice he mentioned feelings of disgust and nausea that overtook him when he contemplated their misery. Perhaps he did not think of himself as a Jew in the same way that they were Jews; he was a Marxist, a convinced internationalist, a man who resisted any narrow, parochial appeal in the name of a universal, political faith. But he had still been born and raised as a Jew. Perhaps the starkness of their lives touched something so deep inside his emotional life that he needed to vomit it out, to disgorge it before it compelled him to see himself in their faces. At moments like these, Leon Trotsky was a Jew in spite of himself.

Years after the Balkan Wars and the Beilis case, Trotsky witnessed worse incidents of hatred directed against the Jews, including large-scale pogroms during the Russian Civil War and the demagogic attacks of Hitler and the Nazis. But he never again invoked the same plain language of disgust. He continued to refer to the Beilis case in his writings. In the last year of his life, in 1939, after Stalin had orchestrated the Great Terror and as Hitler's bellicose intentions became increasingly clear, Trotsky invoked the image of Mendel Beilis. "Retrospectively, in the light of civilization's latest achievements, especially in Germany and the U.S.S.R., [the Beilis] trial today seems almost a humanitarian experiment." With Europe on the verge of a monstrous calamity, Trotsky could think of no better way to personify the continent's suffering than to invoke the image of a poor, lonely Jew falsely accused of killing a Christian child.

Even as he threw himself into his work as a journalist, Trotsky remained intensely involved within party circles. In the summer of 1912 he made another fruitless attempt to promote unity. By that time, the Bolsheviks had revived their underground work within Russia; the Mensheviks were weak, their ranks split among various marginalized groups. Trotsky invited followers of Lenin and of Martov to a conference in Vienna, hoping to initiate a productive dialogue. But Lenin and the Bolsheviks refused to attend. So Trotsky assembled a disparate group of Mensheviks, disaffected Bolsheviks, members of the Jewish Bund, and followers of his own. They called themselves the August Bloc. Here again, Trotsky misread the mood within the ranks of Social Democracy. Lenin was happy with the split in the party; the Mensheviks, who were not interested in reconciling with him either, played along with Trotsky's efforts. They feigned interest in dialogue and unity, leaving it to Trotsky to complain about Lenin's stubborn arrogance. The episode reinforced his frustration with Lenin, with émigré politics in general, and his isolation within the movement. But he was not about to quit the cause of revolution.

In early 1913, in Vienna, Trotsky crossed paths with Joseph Stalin for the first time. Trotsky was visiting a friend from his Viennese *Pravda* days, Matvei Skobelev, a Menshevik who had been elected to the Duma shortly before. They were discussing the overthrow of the tsar over tea when, as Trotsky wrote many years later,

> without a warning knock, the door suddenly opened and an unfamiliar figure appeared on the threshold. He was not very tall, thin, with a dark, gray, colorless face, on which traces of smallpox could be seen. He carried an empty glass. Evidently, he had not expected to meet me and there was nothing friendly in his expression. He made a guttural noise, which could have been taken as a greeting, went to the samovar, silently poured himself some tea, and silently stepped out.

Skobelev explained that this was Djugashvili, that he was from the Caucasus, and that he had just been named to the Bolshevik Central Committee, where he was making a name for himself. Trotsky may have colored his recollection, but there seems nothing false about this brief portrait. At that time, Stalin had just begun editing the Bolshevik *Pravda* and would not have been friendly to Trotsky, who was still engaged in polemical debates with Lenin. Stalin had already expressed his contempt for Trotsky as just another useless intellectual. It was also not in Stalin's nature to be solicitous of another figure in the party unless he believed that he could gain something. Knowing his role in the 1905 revolution and having seen Trotsky debate at the party congress in 1907, Stalin could well have sensed that this was a man he would have either to charm or to challenge—it was too early to decide which.

It is curious that Trotsky waited until 1939 to describe this first meeting. He did not include it in his memoirs or in his biography of Stalin, but wrote about it in an essay called "Hitler's New Friend" in September 1939, shortly after the signing of Molotov-Ribbentrop Nonaggression Pact, when the two dictators agreed to divide Poland between them, allowing Hitler to invade Poland from the west and begin World War II. By 1939 their mutual hatred, and Stalin's murderous attacks on Trotsky's sons and broader family, no doubt loosened Trotsky's restraints. Trotsky never liked to ascribe historical events to the personalities of major figures; it contradicted his Marxist beliefs. Perhaps he was reluctant to connect Stalin's personal behavior—his boorish and sullen conduct, his physical deformities—to the tragic fate of the revolution.

On June 28, 1914, Gavrilo Princip, a young Bosnian Serb, assassinated Archduke Franz Ferdinand, the heir to the throne of the Austro-Hungarian Empire. Six weeks later, Europe was at war, entangled in alliances that brought Italy, Germany, and the Austro-Hungarian Empire into conflict with Russia, France, and England. Trotsky was in Vienna when he heard the news on August 3. He walked around the center of town dismayed by crowds of people aglow with patriotic enthusiasm "for the business of mutual extermination." Their mood reminded him of Saint Petersburg during the general strike of

1905. "No wonder," he wrote in *My Life*, "that in history war has often been the mother of revolution." Other news was equally disheartening; Jean Jaurès had been assassinated in a Paris café by a French nationalist at the end of July. Jaurès, the eloquent defender of Dreyfus, the intellectual champion of French socialism, the founder of *L'Humanité*, and a determined antimilitarist, had worked to avert the war, trying to organize strikes in Germany and France to prevent the conflict. Trotsky had come to know and admire Jaurès. Now his voice was gone.

Trotsky had little time to mourn. As a citizen of Russia living in Austria, he was an enemy alien; alerted to the likelihood of internment, he and his family fled within three hours to Zurich in neutral Switzerland, leaving behind seven years' worth of books and unfinished writings. The next day Trotsky received another shock. By a vote in the Reichstag, the German Social Democrats dropped their opposition to war. Their previous commitment to peace and internationalism was over. Trotsky was not exaggerating when he wrote that the capitulation of the German Social Democrats was one of the "tragic experiences of my life." It set the stage for much of his thinking and action, pitting him against so-called social patriots who supported their own governments in the war. Many of them were longtime colleagues in the ranks of Europe's socialist parties. Once again, Trotsky was not afraid to go it alone.

He stayed in Switzerland for two months. It was a natural refuge for Russian revolutionaries; Nikolai Bukharin and Lenin made their way there, and Trotsky first encountered the German communist Karl Radek in Zurich. Radek had been expelled from Germany for his outspoken antimilitarist views. Trotsky made a vivid impression in Zurich, where Swiss socialists welcomed his denunciation of other European socialists who were now supporting one side or the other. Stirred by the debates swirling around him, Trotsky wrote his influential pamphlet *The War and the International*.

Impatient with all Social Democrats who supported the war, Trotsky reserved particular scorn for the German party. He could not tolerate their triumphant chauvinism or their self-serving argument: that by fighting Russia, Germany had accepted a progressive historical mission. "In our struggle against tsardom," Trotsky insisted, "in which we know no truce, we have not sought and are not seeking assistance from the militarism of the Habsburgs or the Hohenzollerns." It was necessary to reject "the injection of imperialist poison into the German and Austrian proletariat." Socialists should stand for peace, but not a peace to maintain the status quo or allow the contending alliances of capitalist states and empires to work out a different balance of power over the bodies of dead soldiers and workers. Trotsky called for a democratic peace, which would prohibit annexations and guarantee the self-determination of the smaller nations trapped within imperialist empires. In his memoirs, Trotsky was pleased to report that three years later, after the Bolshevik Revolution of 1917, an American publisher brought out his pamphlet in an English translation. It caught the attention of President Woodrow Wilson, who was at the time working on his Fourteen Points. According to Trotsky, Wilson was astonished that a Marxist revolutionary anticipated many of the principles expressed in his own plan for postwar Europe.

But then Trotsky went further, in a direction that Wilson could never approve. In *The War and the International*, Trotsky predicted that the conflict would lead to the collapse of the capitalist system and the nation-state as it had come to be known. "We, revolutionary socialists, did not want war," Trotsky wrote. "But neither are we afraid of it." Disillusioned by the war and its destruction, the international proletariat would choose the path of socialist revolution to forge "a new, more powerful and stable fatherland—the republican United States of Europe, as a transition to the United States of the World."

It was here, however haltingly, that the views of Trotsky and Lenin began to converge. Like Trotsky, Lenin foresaw that the war would bring about profound dislocations and possibly hasten revolution. And as Trotsky had suggested, Lenin conceded that based on "the unevenness of economic and political development" an upheaval in Russia could take place before it spread to Europe. They also shared the belief that for such a revolution to succeed—in a country that had barely advanced past feudalism—it would need the support of the revolutionary parties that would inevitably take power in the rest of the continent.

In the opening months of the war, this debate must have seemed easy to dismiss as the murmuring of shadowy figures on the margins of great events. But well before the vast extent of the carnage became apparent, Trotsky and Lenin understood that this war would change Europe forever. Many others, from diplomats to erstwhile socialist allies, were optimists, blithely predicting that the war would be over within months. Trotsky and Lenin knew better. For them, it was always a senseless slaughter.

Trotsky left Switzerland for France in November, assuming the role of war correspondent for *Kievskaya Mysl*. His family joined him in May 1915, and they settled together on the western outskirts of Paris. For a time, Trotsky divided his work between writing for *Kievskaya Mysl* and collaborating on *Golos* (The voice), a daily Russian émigré newspaper that the Menshevik leader Yuli Martov was editing. *Golos* shared Trotsky's opposition to the war. Even Lenin made note of the newspaper's refusal to tolerate the social patriotism of other Social Democrats. Seeing Lenin and Martov in agreement, both angry with Georgy Plekhanov—who supported Russia against Germany, claiming that German and Austrian monarchs were the true enemies of democratic progress and socialism—Trotsky hoped that unity could finally be established within Russian Social Democracy. But opposition to the war proved not to be a sufficient reason for Bolsheviks and Mensheviks to unite. Martov, for one, did not share Lenin's belief that socialists should call for the defeat of their own countries. Lenin was calling for civil war; Martov was hoping for peace. As they debated among themselves, *Golos* was closed in early January 1915, only to be reborn under the name *Nashe Slovo* (Our word) two weeks later. This time, Trotsky joined Martov as joint editor.

At first glance, *Nashe Slovo* was not an imposing newspaper. Rarely more than four pages long, its pages frequently marred by blank spaces (indicating the work of French military censors), the newspaper had an outsize influence nonetheless. Trotsky and Martov lent its pages to figures who would soon play substantial roles in Russia's fate. Vladimir Antonov-Ovseenko is credited with founding the newspaper; he later led the assault on the Winter Palace in October 1917 and the arrest of the Provisional Government. Solomon Lozovsky headed the Soviet trade union movement during the 1920s and served as deputy foreign minister during World War II. Anatoly Lunacharsky became the first Soviet commissar of education; Alexandra Kollontai became commissar of social welfare; and Ivan Maisky had a distinguished career as a diplomat, serving in London as Soviet ambassador at the height of World War II. (Once Stalin took power, several of them, whether they had been Bolsheviks or Mensheviks, were arrested and destroyed.) Strong personalities, they debated how, as socialists, they should respond to the conflict. Trotsky solicited their views, weighed his own options, and found himself increasingly drawn to Lenin's consistent antimilitarist position. He did not join the Bolsheviks, but he could not conceal from himself that the Bolsheviks came the closest to expressing his own views.

A year into the conflict, socialists were still debating how to proceed against the war. In early September 1915, thirty-eight delegates from eleven countries in Europe gathered in the small Swiss village of Zimmerwald, outside of Bern, for the first international socialist conference since the outbreak of fighting. Swiss laws prohibited citizens of belligerent countries to be in contact, so it required some courage for them to organize the meeting. Trotsky and Lenin both attended, and each played major roles. Lenin, as expected, insisted that socialists should call for the defeat of their own governments and struggle to turn the imperialist war into a civil war in which the proletariat would triumph. Trotsky again found himself leaning in Lenin's direction, and as the delegates debated, they turned to Trotsky to summarize their conclusions. In the end, though, Lenin's position remained in the minority, and the Zimmerwald Manifesto, which Trotsky composed, reflected his remaining differences with the Bolshevik leader. It did not appeal for a civil war, for example. But the Zimmerwald Manifesto did call on workers throughout Europe to abandon support of their own governments and work for a peace "without annexations or war indemnities." As the manifesto declared in Trotsky's words:

> The war has lasted for more than a year. Millions of corpses lie upon the battlefields; millions of men have been crippled for life. Europe has become a gigantic human slaughterhouse. All science, the work of many generations, is devoted to destruction. The most savage barbarity is celebrating its triumph over everything that was previously the pride of mankind.

Lenin and Trotsky both signed the manifesto. But Lenin then issued a statement criticizing the manifesto for failing to clarify "the methods of fighting against the war." Even as it stood, the Zimmerwald Manifesto stirred opposition. The governments of France and Germany suppressed news coverage of the conference, fearing that its appeal could undercut support for the war and its sacrifices. It took another three years of fighting before Germany sued for peace.

Following the conference, Lenin remained in Switzerland and Trotsky returned to France. Their reconciliation was still not complete. Trotsky resumed writing for *Nashe Slovo* and began to devote more time to covering the fighting on the Western Front for *Kievskaya Mysl*. He traveled throughout France, interviewed wounded soldiers, mingled with French and British troops in the squares and cafés of small towns. In descriptions of trench warfare, portraits of individual soldiers, and prescient analyses of how the French thought they could rely on massive defense battlements to safeguard a border, Trotsky conveyed his true feelings about the futility of the war.

In spite of his caution, though, Trotsky was a marked man in France. *Nashe Slovo* continued to appear, although because of French censorship, nothing published could offend official sensibilities. But as Russia dispatched soldiers to the Western Front, it solicited assistance from France; having a revolutionary like Trotsky there was incompatible with the presence of Russian troops on her soil. Right-wing newspapers denounced the editors of *Nashe Slovo* as pro-German; Trotsky was convinced that the articles were planted by Russian diplomats. In September 1916 the French government ordered Trotsky out of the country. He was able to extend his stay while looking for somewhere willing to accept him. He feared being detained and deported to Russia, where his escape from Siberia a decade earlier made him vulnerable to life imprisonment. But after six weeks, the French police lost their patience. Trotsky was physically expelled to Spain. Accompanied by two policemen, he was taken to the southwest corner of France, past Biarritz, and allowed to slip into Spain; from San Sebastián he took a train on his own to Madrid. Trotsky did not speak Spanish and he knew no one in Spain. As he recalled in his memoirs, "I could not have been lonelier even in the Sahara or in the Peter and Paul Fortress." He passed the time visiting museums and reading Spanish newspapers with the aid of a dictionary.

Spanish officials proved equally fearful. Alerted to Trotsky's presence by their counterparts in Paris, the police detained him. Convinced that his ideas were "too advanced for Spain," they dispatched him under guard to Cádiz with a promise to send him to Havana on the next boat. But Trotsky had resources of his own. He was allowed to send telegrams to his supporters, and he managed to get permission for his family to join him in Barcelona, whence they would embark for New York. After seven weeks in Spain, he left for the New World on the rickety steamer *Monserrat*. "The sea was very rough and our boat did everything to remind us of the frailty of human life," he wrote years later. But at least it carried the neutral flag of Spain, lending it a modicum of protection from German submarines. His fellow passengers included wealthy deserters from various countries along with a mix of "undesirables" who were being thrown out of Europe just as he was. The trip took seventeen days; they landed in New York—"a wet mountain of buildings," he called it—on a cold, rainy Saturday.* It was January 13, 1917. Trotsky stayed for only ten weeks, but they were among the most fateful days in the history of both Russia and the United States.

Once in New York, Trotsky found himself drawn to Russian-speaking socialists like himself. Nikolai Bukharin was already there, having been expelled from Scandinavia. Trotsky saw Bukharin within a day after his arrival and was soon joining him as an editor for *Novy Mir* (New world), a Russian émigré socialist newspaper with a distinctly antiwar stance. He resumed his profession as a revolutionary socialist, but since America was still neutral, it was "a profession no more reprehensible than that of a bootlegger." He wrote articles and delivered lectures in New York, Philadelphia, and other cities. The Russian-born anarchist Emma Goldman came away im-

*In his memoirs, Trotsky wrote that January 13 was a Sunday.

pressed when she heard him speak: "After several rather dull speakers Trotsky was introduced," she wrote in her memoirs. "A man of medium height, with haggard cheeks, reddish hair, and straggling red beard stepped briskly forward. His speech, first in Russian and then in German, was powerful and electrifying."* This was the common reaction to a speech by Trotsky.

Living in a small apartment in the Bronx, on East 164th Street and Stebbins Avenue, Trotsky and his family came to enjoy conveniences unheard of for a working-class home in Europe: electric lights, a gas oven, a bath, an automatic elevator, even a chute for the garbage. His sons especially enjoyed the telephone, a device that had not existed in their homes in Vienna and Paris.

As part of his daily routine, Trotsky liked to frequent the Triangle Dairy Restaurant on Wilkins Avenue in the East Bronx, where most of the waiters were Russian Jewish émigrés like himself. As they soon learned to their chagrin, Trotsky had a peculiar view about their profession and its rewards. Trotsky was convinced that "tipping was demeaning to the dignity of a workingman, and that a person should get a regular salary, enough to live on, and not have to depend on tips." As a matter of principle, he refused to leave a tip himself and would harangue other customers to do the same. Such behavior did not endear him to the waiters; they all tried to avoid serving him. They also took to calling him "Leo Fonfatch," a play on the Yiddish word for speaking through one's nose (*fonfend*); the way Trotsky spoke, they thought he suffered from sinus trouble or adenoids.

The waiters conspired against him. As one after another refused to serve him, he "was shifted from one waiter's station to another, abused, shouted at, ignored, even had hot soup

---

*Notwithstanding Emma Goldman's description, Trotsky had a dark beard and hair.

spilled on him." Finally, a new waiter took pity on Trotsky. He would serve him promptly and Trotsky, out of appreciation, would eat quickly, then leave, allowing a more generous customer to sit down. Still, he refused to leave a tip for his benefactor. This same waiter tried to dissuade Trotsky from returning to Russia, to "forget his *meshugana* dreams of overthrowing the tsar." Trotsky saw things differently.

This modest episode highlights a paradox at the heart of Trotsky's attitude toward his Jewish identity. Although he was estranged from a sense of himself as a Jew, he still gravitated to Jews wherever he lived. Perhaps it was a matter of convenience—if they were from Russia, they spoke his mother tongue—or perhaps it was a matter of familiarity: once outside of Russia he sought the company of people like himself.

Soon after arriving in New York, Trotsky was welcomed by Abraham Cahan, the legendary editor of the *Forverts* (Forward), a Yiddish-language daily with a wide readership in the Jewish immigrant community. Cahan and his colleagues were socialists; they were thrilled to meet Trotsky. The *Forverts* ran an interview with him on January 16; soon after, it ran four columns by Trotsky. All the pieces reflected his internationalist stance and his criticism of the war and the Allies. Resentful over his expulsion from Paris, he naturally targeted France, claiming that it was subservient to the tsar. He denied he was pro-German, in spite of the fact that the *Forverts*, like the vast majority of its Russian Jewish readers, took a pro-German stance, hoping to see the downfall of the tsarist autocracy. Without the constraints of military censorship, Trotsky threw caution to the wind. In one article he went so far as to counsel American workers to choose between internationalism and patriotism. "It is necessary to consciously choose between these two directions, which are incompatible for those Americans, and especially the Jewish American workers, who have failed to make the choice until now." Regardless of their interest in socialism, it is hard to imagine many Russian Jews in New York, having reached the *goldene medineh* (Yiddish for the "golden country"), deciding to choose sides against America in the name of revolutionary socialism.

Furthermore, Trotsky's articles appeared at a time when Wilson's government was heading to a confrontation with Imperial Germany. America had declared its neutrality immediately after the outbreak of hostilities and Wilson had won re-election in 1916, pledging to keep the country out of Europe's war. But events were compelling him to reconsider. At the end of January 1917, Germany declared unrestricted submarine warfare. Its strategy was clear. The German high command believed it could break the British naval blockade and punish England sufficiently before the United States could enter the war. But then Germany made a foolish miscalculation. That same January, British cryptographers deciphered a telegram from the German foreign minister Arthur Zimmermann to the German ambassador in Mexico. He was offering Mexico an audacious proposal: in return for a Mexican declaration of war against the United States, Germany would encourage Mexico to "reconquer lost territory in Texas, New Mexico, and Arizona." In order to protect their intelligence methods from detection, the British waited until February 24 to inform the White House; the American press covered the story on March 1. The Zimmermann telegram marked a turning point in the war. Anti-German feeling, which was already growing after the sinking of the American passenger ship *Lusitania* in May 1915, came to a boil.

Neutrality was no longer possible, and any pro-German feeling on the part of Russian Jews in New York came to an end. The *Forverts* responded accordingly. It carried a front-page announcement that "if Germany can really commit such an idiotic move of diplomacy, then every citizen of America will fight to the last drop of his blood to protect the great

American republic." Trotsky could not abide such a bellicose stance. He was opposed to the war and any hint of American entry. Trotsky continued to believe that faced with the choice of supporting an antimilitarist stance or defending the United States, American Jews, and Russian émigrés in particular, should resist any patriotic appeals.

History, though, had another surprise. As strikes and urban unrest spread in Russia, fueled by food shortages and the ongoing, disastrous war, word reached Europe and America that Tsar Nicholas II had abdicated on March 2. Begun in 1613, the Romanov dynasty was finished; the Provisional Government, led by Western-oriented liberal parties, took power hoping to resolve Russia's urgent dilemmas.

Trotsky was determined to return to Russia. He followed events as best he could. Seeing liberals in charge, he denounced the Mensheviks for lending their support. Trotsky was sure that the end of the autocracy and the ensuing power struggle would be matched by revolutions in Europe, most probably in Germany. He could not envision a different future. On March 20, he addressed a gathering at the Harlem Casino in upper Manhattan. A Russian-language notice in the *Forverts* announced a "mass meeting" about "Revolution in Russia." "Speakers in Yiddish, Russian, English and other languages. L. N. Trotsky will speak in Russian. Admission is free."*

America, too, would have to be challenged. On the night of March 26, just as he was preparing to leave, he addressed a rally in Manhattan, stirring the crowd with a call for revolution: "I want you people to organize and keep on organizing until you are able to overthrow the damned, rotten, capitalistic government of this country." Two years later, during a Senate hearing about Bolshevik propaganda, a witness to Trotsky's speech in New York described him "as a typical Russian; black, bushy,

*The notice should have read "L. D. Trotsky" for Lev Davidovich.

curly hair, and very radical looking in appearance as well as in speech."*

His departure the next day seemed uneventful. Trotsky and his family left New York aboard the Norwegian liner *Christianiafjord*. His papers were all in order; he had a British transit visa and an entry permit issued by a compliant Russian consul. He left America "with the feeling of a man who has had only a peep into the foundry in which the fate of man is to be forged." America had placed its mark on him, but as hard as he tried to return, destiny and recalcitrant American officials prevented that from happening.

Just days out of New York, the ship was stopped and boarded by British officials in Halifax, Nova Scotia. Trotsky and his family were removed; he was arrested and sent to a camp for German prisoners of war in nearby Amherst, while his wife and children were allowed to stay in Halifax. The British, anxious to keep Russia in the war, were acting under instruction from nervous officials in Petrograd, as Saint Petersburg had been renamed at the beginning of the war. It would be imprudent to permit a revolutionary like Trotsky to return home. Other passengers protested on his behalf to the British, but Trotsky, true to his principles, refused to do so. He did not see the point of "complaining to Beelzebub about Satan."

The British held him for more than three weeks. As might be expected, Trotsky proved a difficult prisoner. He turned the camp of eight hundred German POWs into "one continuous mass-meeting," explaining in speeches and smaller discussions that the war was a crime. So many prisoners followed his every word that German officers appealed to the British to prohibit him from talking to the POWs, a request the warden was

*Trotsky was such a prominent speaker in radical circles in New York that a corner north of Central Park was nicknamed "Trotsky's Corner" in honor of his eloquence.

happy to grant. In Russia, meanwhile, word of his arrest provoked indignant protests and led to his eventual release. Trotsky was let go on April 29, as exultant German sailors and the sounds of the "Internationale" accompanied him to the gates.

It took Trotsky and his family almost three weeks to reach Sweden. From there they traveled to Finland and then on to Russia, reaching Petrograd on May 17. The tsar had stepped down ten weeks before. Lenin had returned on April 3, and like Lenin, Trotsky arrived by train at the Finland Station. A crowd was there to greet him. He called for a second revolution in the name of the workers, but could barely finish his thoughts when hands lifted him in the air. He had returned once before to Saint Petersburg in 1905, led a failed revolution, and then escaped the country, not knowing when or how he would go back. Now he was home. Another revolution was at hand.

4

The Revolution of 1917

SPEAKING BEFORE TSARIST JUDGES in 1905, Trotsky declared, "A popular insurrection cannot be staged. It can only be foreseen." Twenty-five years later, in forced exile and anxious to defend the role he had played in the Bolshevik takeover, Trotsky wrote his *History of the Russian Revolution.* Caught between the urge to sustain the Bolshevik claim that the masses had inspired the seizure of power and the unavoidable truth of his and Lenin's fundamental roles, Trotsky wavered. He emphasized the inevitable momentum of events—"Revolution is the inspired frenzy of history," he wrote in *My Life*—and the contingent need for Bolshevik leadership. He could not claim otherwise. History, in the end, will have to agree with the more candid admission in his diary of 1935. "Had I not been present in 1917 in Petersburg, the October Revolution would still have taken place—*on the condition that Lenin was present and in command* [translator's italics]. If neither Lenin nor I had been present in Petersburg, there would have been no October Revolution." The revolution might have been made without Trotsky, but it needed both Lenin and Trotsky to succeed.

In May 1917 Trotsky returned to a Russia in turmoil. The tsar had abdicated in the wake of violent demonstrations, industrial strikes, and mutinies by soldiers and sailors. Protests over lack of bread turned into a revolution. The Petrograd Soviet of Workers' Deputies, which had once been led by Trotsky, declared its revival. On March 1 the Soviet issued its famous Order No. 1, granting soldiers democratic rights and calling on officers to treat them with greater respect. The next day, the Provisional Government assumed power in Petrograd, leaving Tsar Nicholas II no choice but to abdicate.

Russia seemed poised to establish a parliamentary republic. The Provisional Government represented the coming to power of a potentially democratic Russia. It guaranteed civil liberties and removed all restrictions on Russia's minorities, most notably by abolishing the Pale of Settlement and granting Jews equal status before the law. Its first prime minister was Prince Georgy Lvov, a member of a noble family with deep roots in the country's history. Like other Kadets, he had a strong regard for liberal, Western values. The tsar had abdicated in favor of his brother, Grand Duke Mikhail Alexandrovich, and there was some support within the Provisional Government to honor the tsar's wishes. But the grand duke refused the appointment. The revolution would not be confined to the removal of Nicholas II.

With the tsar gone, followers of the monarchy and other conservative parties vanished from the political scene. In the ensuing revolutionary situation, liberal parties like the Kadets dominated the Provisional Government and made up the country's right wing. Socialist parties, including the Bolsheviks, Mensheviks, and Socialist Revolutionaries, constituted the left. They led the Petrograd Soviet and offered conditional support to the Provisional Government, including for the war effort, convinced that the peasants—who made up the majority of Russia's population—still hoped for victory.

Leaders of these revolutionary parties hurried to the capital, some from Siberian exile, others from Europe and America. With the collapse of tsarist rule, they regained their freedom of movement. Lenin's arrival on the night of April 3 marked a turning point. Lenin was living in Zurich when the tsar abdicated, and wanted to return immediately, but he had to find a way across German lines. At the same time, the Provisional Government was reluctant to accept his presence in Russia. After weeks of negotiation, Lenin arranged with the German general staff for a train to carry him and dozens of colleagues to Petrograd. This was the famous sealed train. It consisted of one carriage; the Germans would not inspect passports or luggage. Lenin wanted to see Russia withdraw from the conflict, a position that suited Kaiser Wilhelm's purposes.

Lenin's arrival galvanized the Bolsheviks. It also confused them. On the train, he had formulated a new strategy for his party. Since the downfall of the monarchy, most of the Bolsheviks had offered support to the Provisional Government. Lenin saw things differently. The day after his arrival, he attended an assembly of Social Democrats, a meeting designed to discuss reunification between Bolsheviks and Mensheviks. It was held in the Tauride Palace, where both the Petrograd Soviet and the Provisional Government maintained offices. Lenin presented his famous April Theses to a stunned audience: the Bolsheviks should no longer support the Provisional Government and must break with the Mensheviks. All power should be in the hands of the Soviets, who could then end the war and reorganize the country along socialist principles. Lenin stopped short of calling for Russia's defeat; if he were to trumpet it aloud, the Bolshevik Party could be declared illegal and forced underground.

Lenin intended to undermine the Provisional Government. Social Democrats had believed, in line with a traditional understanding of Marxist theory, that Russia must experience a bourgeois, democratic revolution, accompanied by industrialization and a growing class of urban workers, before the proletariat could seize power. But now Lenin was declaring, however indirectly, that Russia was ready for a full-blown dictatorship of the proletariat; as in 1905, the middle class was not poised to complete a democratic revolution, while the war reinforced the likelihood of socialist revolutions in Western Europe. Lenin was beginning to sound like Trotsky. Trotsky, too, had quickly denounced the Provisional Government while he was in New York. As Lenin moved closer to calling for a takeover by the proletariat, his ideas echoed Trotsky's call for permanent revolution. Alert to this comparison, some Bolsheviks condemned the April Theses as "Trotskyite."

Nonetheless, Lenin and Trotsky could not easily reconcile. After Trotsky reached Petrograd on May 4, he did not see Lenin for several days. Once he placed his family in a boarding house, he headed for the Tauride Palace and a session of the Petrograd Soviet. His colleagues—Mensheviks, Bolsheviks, and Socialist Revolutionaries—were not sure how to receive him. According to Angela Balabanoff, the secretary of the Zimmerwald movement and a longtime friend, they "regarded him with rancor and distrust . . . partly out of fear of competition." But he could not be denied standing. As the Bolsheviks pointed out, the chairman of the 1905 Soviet ought to have a leadership role in the new Soviet; Trotsky was made an associate member of the Executive Committee, but without the right to vote.

Trotsky initially aligned himself with a small group of intellectual Social Democrats. Frustrated over the endless debates that arose in exile, many, like Trotsky, had found themselves estranged from both Bolsheviks and Mensheviks. They called themselves the Inter-Borough Organization. But now, opposed to the war and the policies of the Provisional Government, the group considered joining the Bolsheviks. They soon met with Lenin, and it became apparent to him and to Trotsky that their views were converging. But Trotsky still hesitated to join the party and relinquish his independence.

Their personal differences also contributed to Trotsky's reluctance. By temperament, Lenin and Trotsky were almost complete opposites. Lenin had a distinct puritanical streak, devoting all his energy to the cause of revolution. He lived simply, read only books that contributed to his work, and did his best to avoid sentimental pleasures. He once remarked about himself after hearing a performance of Beethoven's *Appassionata Sonata* that he "must not listen to music too often. It makes me want to say kind, stupid things, and pat the heads of people."

Trotsky was not like this at all. Although he did not smoke and almost always avoided liquor, he enjoyed art and music, read widely in several languages, raised children with his second wife, and adored hunting and fishing. While Lenin dressed like a clerk, Trotsky, who did not restrain his self-regard, always dressed like a meticulous, bourgeois gentleman. Lenin was intelligent, but his genius was limited to political action; he had a one-track mind. Bertrand Russell met Lenin in 1920 and came away "chiefly conscious of his intellectual limitations and his rather narrow Marxian orthodoxy." Lenin appalled him. Trotsky, in contrast, had a capacious enthusiasm for learning. He wrote on literature and culture, on science and technology. As we have seen, he was a successful journalist and war correspondent.

But the prospect of revolution brought them together. Lenin needed Trotsky's charismatic energy, his ability to inspire a multitude. It was Trotsky, though, who made the more dramatic shift in thinking. During his years of opposition to Lenin, Trotsky had rejected the idea of a vanguard party taking power with the support of the working class. Nonetheless, in the spring and summer of 1917, Trotsky saw the utility of joining forces with Lenin at a moment when a determined party could seize control in a country overwhelmed by turmoil.

It was as an orator that Trotsky asserted his presence particularly at two significant sites in the capital: the large public hall called the Modern Circus and the Kronstadt Naval Base outside of Petrograd, where sailors were in outright rebellion against their officers. The Provisional Government wanted to impose discipline on the men. Trotsky defended the sailors, insisting that "should a counterrevolutionary general try to throw a noose around the neck of the revolution, . . . the Kronstadt sailors will come and fight and die with us." He often met with them, forging ties that reinforced their faith in socialism. Of all the revolutionary leaders, Trotsky was the closest to the Kronstadt sailors.

It was at the Modern Circus, though, that Trotsky mesmerized the crowds. "Life was a whirl of enormous rallies," he wrote in his memoirs. "Rallies were held in plants, schools, and colleges, in theaters, circuses, streets, and squares." No speaker was more sought after than he. On almost any night at the Modern Circus, "every square inch was filled," Trotsky recalled. The crowds were "like infants clinging with their dry lips to the nipples of the revolution."

> I made my way to the platform through a narrow human trench, sometimes I was borne overhead. The air, intense with breathing and waiting, fairly exploded with shouts and with the passionate yells peculiar to the Modern Circus. Above and around me was a press of elbows, chests, and heads. I spoke from out of a warm cavern of human bodies; whenever I stretched out my hands I would touch someone, and a grateful movement in response would give me to understand that I was not to worry about it, not to break off my speech, but keep on. No speaker, no matter how exhausted, could resist the electric tension of that impassioned human throng.

Trotsky saw his teenage daughters, Zinaida and Nina, in the Modern Circus. They were living nearby with their mother. "I would barely manage to beckon to them, in answer to their excited glances, or to press their warm hands on the way out," he wrote in *My Life*. He had abandoned them in 1902, but they had been raised to admire him.

Trotsky's speeches confirmed his preeminence. The veteran Bolshevik Anatoly Lunacharsky described Trotsky's compelling eloquence: his "mighty rhythm of speech, loud absolutely tireless voice, wonderful compactness, literariness of phrase, wealth of imagery, scorching irony, flowing pathos, an absolutely extraordinary logic." Trotsky projected a defiant urge for revolution, while Lenin, often keeping in the background, kept his gaze on the inner workings of the party. They were now partners in revolution, their ideas and personalities complementing each other. "I came to Lenin fighting," Trotsky once told Max Eastman, "but I came unreservedly and all the way."

That spring, the Bolsheviks continued to press their erstwhile socialist allies. In June the First All-Russian Congress of the Soviets gathered in the capital, where it met for three weeks. Lenin and Trotsky attended and lost no time in badgering moderate Mensheviks and Socialist Revolutionaries over their willingness to support the Provisional Government.* These parties now commanded a large majority in the country, but still deferred to the liberals, allowing Prince Lvov and others to keep Russia in the war and avoid satisfying the peasants' demand for land. "The war dragged on aimlessly, ceaselessly, and interminably," Trotsky wrote. "The government took no steps whatever to extricate itself from the vicious circle." Trotsky yearned for another revolution, this time by and for the

---

*Alexander Kerensky, whose government would be overthrown by Lenin and Trotsky in October, met them for the first and only time at this Congress.

proletariat. Lenin had similar aims. In early June the Bolsheviks announced plans to stage a large demonstration in Petrograd to challenge both the Provisional Government and the
Soviet. There were unsettling fears that the demonstrators
would be armed and might move to take control of the city.
Under pressure from the Congress of Soviets, Lenin was compelled to back down and cancel the demonstration. But others
came away from the episode convinced that Lenin had been
trying to mount "a conspiracy to overthrow the government,"
because the Bolsheviks knew, in the words of the Menshevik
leader Irakli Tsereteli, that "they will never come to power any
other way." That month Trotsky addressed a group of revolutionary sailors in a public square. "The strength of the French
Revolution was in the machine that made the enemies of the
people shorter by a head," Trotsky shouted. "This is a fine device. We must have it in every city." And have it they did.

History speeded up that summer, and not to the Bolsheviks' advantage. While the Congress of the Soviets was in session, the Russian army went on the offensive in Galicia. The
Eastern Front had been quiet since the tsar's abdication; the
armies of Austria and Germany were waiting for Russia's to
collapse. But the minister of war, Alexander Kerensky, who was
a leading figure in the Socialist Revolutionary party and the
dominant man in the Provisional Government, rallied the army
to attack with the hope that *democratic* Russian forces in a post-
tsarist country would triumph over the armies of discredited
monarchies. He made a tragic miscalculation. The offensive
collapsed. Russian units were either routed or retreated in
haste, defying their officers and abandoning their positions.
For Trotsky, the offensive confirmed the Provisional Government's hopeless leadership.

This dramatic defeat, together with worsening economic
conditions, led to an unexpected upheaval, which historians
call the July Days. The Provisional Government and the Pet-

rograd Soviet, working together, both were proving to be incapable of resolving Russia's difficult problems. Out of frustration, crowds of workers, soldiers, and sailors took to the streets calling for an all-socialist government. They demanded that the moderate socialist parties abandon their coalition with the Kadets and take power on their own. Inspired by Bolshevik slogans for an end to the war and more radical economic and social reforms, a crowd besieged the Tauride Palace. Their target was both the Provisional Government and the Menshevik and Socialist Revolutionary leaders who refused to break with it.

Historians still debate whether Lenin and Trotsky were planning to seize power at that moment. Most accounts confirm that the demonstrations caught them by surprise. Lenin was resting in Finland. Trotsky remained in Petrograd and was in the Tauride Palace when the crowds descended. The minister of agriculture, Viktor Chernov, who was a leader of the Socialist Revolutionary Party, was seized outside the building and forced into a car. The crowd, led by unruly sailors from Kronstadt, appeared eager to lynch him. Trotsky rushed to Chernov's defense. "You are the pride and glory of the revolution," he shouted. "You have come here . . . to show the Soviet that the working class does not wish to see the bourgeoisie in power. But why should you harm your own cause?" Trotsky asked. "Why should you obscure and blot your record by mean violence over random individuals?" The crowd remained sullen and hostile. Trotsky challenged them, asking whoever was prepared to hurt Chernov to raise his hand. No one stirred. Sensing the advantage, Trotsky took Chernov by the hand— the poor man was barely conscious from fear—and led him into the Tauride Palace. The whole scene confused and demoralized the crowd. They were in the streets demanding "All power to the Soviets" while Trotsky was saving a Socialist Revolutionary minister from their wrath. In what direction could events be leading? Striking workers still assailed socialist ministers. Kronstadt sailors held the Peter and Paul Fortress. The scale of the turmoil was impressive: up to a half million people took to the streets on July 4. There was looting, there were fights between Bolshevik sympathizers and Black Hundred agitators, even sniper attacks; four hundred people lost their lives. But without leaders to offer a concrete way forward, the demonstrations gradually faded.

Further events undermined Bolshevik standing. The right-wing press published claims that the Bolsheviks were German agents, a charge linked to Lenin's arrival on the sealed train and a rumor that the Bolsheviks had received funds from Germany as well. (This rumor later turned out to be true.) At the same time, news of collapse at the front further aggravated anti-Bolshevik feelings, with generals claiming that the violence in Petrograd had undermined the morale of the army. Suddenly, it was the Bolsheviks who were vulnerable, not the moderate socialists who had been the targets of the demonstrators, and not Kerensky, who had been responsible for the debacle at the front. An order was issued for Lenin's arrest, and he wondered aloud to Trotsky whether they might be shot on sight. *Pravda* was banned, its offices ransacked; workers sympathetic to the Bolsheviks and organized into Red Guard units were disarmed, Bolshevik agitators prevented from speaking to troops. Lenin went into hiding and did not give another public speech until the revolution in October. Trotsky, still at large, publicly defended Lenin and the actions of the Bolsheviks; he even challenged the government to arrest him. Kerensky obliged Trotsky on the night of July 23. He was charged with having returned with Lenin through Germany and with being a member of the Bolshevik Central Committee. Both claims were factually untrue. Trotsky was taken to Kresty, the same prison that had confined him in 1905.

The events of the July Days exposed the weakness of both the Provisional Government and the moderate socialist parties. The entire edifice of the February revolution, all the institutions and parties that had emerged with the fall of the Romanovs, appeared fragile. Confidence in the Provisional Government plummeted. Kerensky could not assemble a stable cabinet of ministers. Within the officer corps, there had always been a mood of resentment over the army's weakened authority and the democratic reforms that in their eyes were ruining Russia. That summer, Kerensky appointed General Lavr Kornilov to be commander in chief. With calls for order resounding throughout the country, many officers wanted Kornilov to impose a military dictatorship.

The Kornilov Affair engulfed Russia for a week in August. It began on August 24 with Kornilov's call to overthrow the Provisional Government as his troops began to march on Petrograd. Kerensky turned to the socialists and the Bolsheviks for support. He restored weapons to the Red Guards and called on the sailors of Kronstadt to defend the revolution. Kornilov's plan quickly collapsed and he was arrested on August 31. Kerensky was the principal loser in this affair, compromised by his appointment of Kornilov and allegations that he had quietly urged the general to act. Kornilov had hoped to crush the radical left. But his defeat had the opposite effect from his intentions: it radicalized the country and set the stage for the Bolsheviks to come to power.

Now the Bolsheviks and their left-wing allies among the Mensheviks and Socialist Revolutionaries benefited from a surge of popularity. Suddenly, the Bolsheviks gained a majority in the Petrograd Soviet and in other city soviets and army committees. Trotsky was released on bail on September 4. He was now officially a Bolshevik; the Inter-Borough Organization had joined with Lenin while Trotsky was in prison, and he had been elected to its Central Committee. While Lenin remained in hiding, Trotsky became the Bolsheviks' chief spokesman; on September 23, the Petrograd Soviet elected him as its president.

Trotsky's initial speech was conciliatory. Chastened by the events of July and Kornilov's attempted putsch, Trotsky spoke modestly. "We are all party men," Trotsky declared, "and more than once we shall clash with one another. But we shall conduct the work of the Petrograd Soviet in a spirit of lawfulness and of full freedom for all parties. The hand of the Presidium will never lend itself to the suppression of a minority." The Bolshevik takeover was a month away. When the time came, Trotsky failed to honor his pledge.

With the country in political disarray, Lenin sensed an opportunity. From his hiding place in Finland, he pressed the party to call for armed insurrection. It would be "utter idiocy or sheer treachery" to miss such a moment, Lenin insisted. But the majority of his colleagues were not ready. Two of his principal comrades, Lev Kamenev and Grigory Zinoviev, argued against seizing power. (Kamenev was married to Trotsky's younger sister, Olga.) They feared the consequences of defeat. Kamenev supported the creation of a broad socialist government; such willingness to work with Mensheviks and Left Socialist Revolutionaries set him and others apart from Lenin. He and Zinoviev wanted to wait for Kerensky to convene the Constituent Assembly, which all the parties of Russia's post-February government claimed to support.

Trotsky offered a different approach. He wanted the appeal for an all-socialist government to come from the Petrograd Soviet, making it easier for hesitant supporters to join them. He advised the Bolsheviks to wait until the Second All-Russia Congress of Soviets, scheduled for October 20, to arrange for the transfer of power; the Bolsheviks, he was confident, would control a majority of the delegates.

Lenin and Trotsky believed that the balance of political forces inside Russia favored the Bolsheviks. Lenin, as well, insisted throughout the fall that revolution was imminent in Europe. Trotsky had long asserted that a proletarian revolution in

Russia would provoke upheavals in the rest of Europe. Now their views were growing closer.

Throughout September and October the country wondered what the Bolsheviks would do; ever since June, Lenin's intention to seize power had been increasingly clear. In Petrograd especially, discontent over the war and the lack of food reinforced support for radical change. In October, German advances began to threaten land and sea approaches to the capital. The Provisional Government wanted to send half of the Petrograd garrison to the front, a move that provoked angry protests from the soldiers, who were among the most determined supporters of the Bolsheviks; they feared that such a move could be part of a counterrevolutionary plot. For months there had been rumors that the government was prepared to move the capital to Moscow and abandon Petrograd to the Germans. Trotsky recognized the compelling logic of such a decision. "For some," he wrote in 1919, "the loss of Petrograd to the Germans would be okay. Under the peace treaty it would be restored, but restored ravaged by German militarism. By that time the revolution would be decapitated, and it would be easier to manage." He moved to prevent any such maneuver. On October 9 the Petrograd Soviet authorized creation of the Military Revolutionary Committee (MRC) to assure defense of the capital. But under Trotsky's leadership, the MRC became the principal vehicle for insurrection.

It was in this atmosphere that Lenin emerged from hiding on October 10 and went to Petrograd to meet with the party's central committee. He had not seen them since July. At his insistence, the party leadership passed a resolution—ten votes to two, with only Kamenev and Zinoviev in dissent—calling for an armed seizure of power by the Bolsheviks. But it gave no specific date for the uprising. The Central Committee also selected its first Political Bureau, including Lenin, Trotsky, Zinoviev, Kamenev, and Stalin. In spite of their opposition views,

Kamenev and Zinoviev were elected to leadership positions, a sign that the party continued to tolerate political diversity within its ranks. Lenin then returned to Finland.

This left Trotsky to lead the forces of revolution. He spoke to workers in Petrograd's largest factories, to soldiers in their barracks, to public meetings throughout the city. "It seemed that he spoke everywhere simultaneously," wrote Nikolai Sukhanov, an active Menshevik, whose memoir of the revolution remains among the most reliable. "Every worker and soldier in Petrograd knew him and listened to him. His influence on the masses and the leaders alike was overwhelming. He was the central figure of those days, and the chief hero of this remarkable chapter of history." With the Congress of Soviets scheduled to convene on October 20, Trotsky was anxious to have sufficient support for the transfer of power. On October 16 the Petrograd garrison voted against following any orders from Kerensky to deploy outside of the capital. That same day, Trotsky ordered that thousands of rifles be issued to the Red Guards; his command was obeyed, confirming the authority of the MRC. Each day was now precious.

Lenin, this time in heavy disguise, came out of hiding to rally the Bolsheviks. He carried a majority in the Central Committee; by vote it tentatively fixed October 20 as the date of the uprising. Kamenev, who remained opposed to seizing power—he and Zinoviev argued that right-wing forces were still strong within the country, while the Bolsheviks and their revolutionary allies were in no position to "declare war on the entire bourgeois world"—resigned from the Central Committee and made clear his intention to alert the public. On October 18 he published an article in Maxim Gorky's newspaper, *Novaya Zhizn* (New life), declaring that "the instigation of an armed uprising before and independent of the Soviet Congress would be an impermissible and even fatal step for the proletariat and the revolution." Rumors about an insurrection had been circulating for some time, but now, with Kamenev's article, there could be no outright denial. Trotsky, nonetheless, insisted to the Petrograd Soviet that no such plan existed; it was a transparent evasion, if not an outright lie. Lenin was beside himself with rage; he denounced both Kamenev and Zinoviev and wanted them expelled from the party. The British ambassador Sir George Buchanan watched these events unfold with unbridled anguish. "I could not understand how a Government that respected itself could allow Trotsky to go on inciting the masses to murder and pillage without arresting him," he wrote in his diary. But Kerensky failed to act.

With the Congress of Soviets approaching and with explicit knowledge of Bolshevik intentions, the Mensheviks and Socialist Revolutionary leaders of the Petrograd Soviet voted to postpone the Congress for five days; they hoped to counter Lenin and Trotsky. But it was the Bolsheviks who benefited from their move. Within days, the MRC asserted its dominance within the city. It confirmed the loyalty of the Petrograd garrison and, thanks to Trotsky's personal intervention, enlisted military units in the Peter and Paul Fortress whose guns could reach the Winter Palace. (A year later, on the first anniversary of the revolution, Stalin praised Trotsky for this step.) Kerensky and his ministers were increasingly defenseless.

On the morning of October 24, Kerensky ordered two Bolshevik newspapers closed; his men destroyed copies of that day's issues and tried to wreck the print beds. Trotsky responded quickly, sending armed workers loyal to the Bolsheviks to guard the offices, while dispatching other units to take control of key points in the city. Kerensky tried to impose his authority by announcing plans to arrest Lenin, Trotsky, and all the leaders of the MRC, and to discipline the sailors of Kronstadt. Such threats led nowhere. Throughout the afternoon, units of soldiers and armed workers under the command of the MRC seized railroad stations and bridges. By the evening, it was the Bolsheviks who controlled Petrograd. There was little if any violence.

Later that night, Fyodor Dan, the leader of the Menshevik Central Executive, tried to forestall the Bolshevik takeover. The American journalist John Reed was in the hall when Dan warned against Bolshevik provocations that could only lead to a right-wing counterattack. Dan promised that the Soviet would now pursue peace negotiations, that it would institute land reform. Voices drowned him out, derisively dismissing his appeals as too little, too late. Then Trotsky took the floor. John Reed captured the moment in *Ten Days That Shook the World:*

> Trotsky mounted the tribune, borne on a wave of roaring applause. . . . His thin, pointed face was positively Mephistophelian in its expression of malicious irony.
>
> "Dan's tactics proved that the masses—the great, dull indifferent masses—are absolutely with him!" (Titanic mirth.) He turned towards the Chairman, dramatically. "When we spoke of giving the land to the peasants you were against it. We told the peasants, 'If they don't give it to you, take it yourselves!' and the peasants followed our advice. And now you advocate what we did six months ago. . . . Dan tells you that you have no right to make an insurrection. Insurrection is the right of all revolutionaries! . . . If you maintain complete confidence, there will be no civil war. Our enemies will surrender at once and you will take the place which is legitimately yours, that of the masters of the Russian land."

By midnight, the Bolsheviks shifted their tactics. Realizing that the Provisional Government was weaker than they had thought, they began to take more aggressive actions. Lenin's arrival reinforced their resolve. He had been hiding in Vyborg, a working-class suburb filled with Bolshevik supporters. In disguise—he wore a wig and a bandage across his face—he arrived at the Bolshevik headquarters in the Smolny Institute (a small palace that had housed an elite boarding school for girls) accompanied by a single bodyguard. Now the MRC began to set up roadblocks and deploy armored cars to patrol the city. They gained control of police stations, the post and telegraph office, the state bank, and the principal electric station. Fearing resistance from reactionaries, they issued an order "to suppress the agitation of the Black Hundred without reserve, and at the first attempts at pogroms on the streets, arms should be used without mercy." But there was little if any turmoil or armed resistance. Only the immediate area around the Winter Palace, where the ministers of the Provisional Government were anxiously meeting, was not in their hands. Lenin and Trotsky announced the successful takeover on the afternoon of October 25, but it was not until early in the morning of the next day that Bolshevik units arrested the government ministers. Kerensky, by then, had fled for the front, hoping to locate loyal troops to stop the Bolsheviks.

While the siege of the Winter Palace was still unfolding, the delayed Congress of Soviets convened on the night of October 25. The political drama that was about to take place was as historically significant as the armed takeover of the city.

The delegates to the Congress numbered more than 650; they represented a broad range of socialist parties, from the most radical Bolsheviks and their allies among the Left Socialist Revolutionaries and the Menshevik-Internationalists to more moderate Mensheviks and Socialist Revolutionaries. The insurrection was being carried out in the name of the Petrograd Soviet, so it was natural for the delegates to assume that the goal of the Congress was to form a broad coalition government of socialist parties. The Bolsheviks controlled 300 seats and counted on the additional support of more than 80 Left Socialist Revolutionaries to give them a majority.

Yuli Martov, speaking for the Menshevik-Internationalists, appealed to the Congress to forge a broad coalition. But other, more moderate delegates objected altogether, condemning the

Bolsheviks for seizing power before the Congress could meet. In their eyes, such action signaled "the beginning of civil war and the breakup of the Constituent Assembly and threatens to destroy the Revolution." With that, many of the Mensheviks and Socialist Revolutionaries left the hall, even declaring the intention to go to the Winter Palace to show solidarity with the Provisional Government. Thanks to their departure, the Bolsheviks alone now commanded an absolute majority in the hall.

Once more, Martov intervened, pleading to avoid civil war by forming a coalition "acceptable to the whole revolutionary democracy." But the Bolsheviks, emboldened by their majority, were in no mood to negotiate. Trotsky dismissed Martov's appeal for compromise in words filled with arrogance and contempt. "Our rising has been victorious. Now they tell us: Renounce your victory, yield, make a compromise. With whom? . . . With these miserable little groups that have left or with those that make these proposals? . . . You are miserable, isolated individuals. You are bankrupt. You have played out your role," he told Martov to his face. "Go where you belong: to the dustbin of history."* Now it was Martov's turn to leave. From that moment on, the Bolsheviks saw their way clear to a one-party dictatorship. In February the Bolshevik party had hardly numbered 25,000 members. Eight months later, it had grown to more than 300,000 and was on the verge of controlling a country of 150 million.

History can be a proud and unforgiving god. Trotsky's dismissal of the Mensheviks, including his old friend Yuli Martov, presaged much of the demagoguery that came to dominate Bolshevik rule. Trotsky was not only rejecting the Mensheviks' more cautious, more tolerant, more liberal understanding of what a socialist revolution must mean; he was also helping— very much helping—to lay the foundation for decades of rule by a ruthless, one-party dictatorship.

*Trotsky used the Russian word *svalka*, which means "town dump."

It was the Bolsheviks' insistence on a monopoly of power that provoked the civil war. Perhaps if they had agreed to a coalition with other revolutionary parties, this might have assuaged right-wing forces. Or perhaps not. The civil war, after all, was initiated by right-wing and pro-monarchist groups. But such a concession would have diminished full Bolshevik control and broadened the space for political dialogue, something Lenin and Trotsky were not about to do.

The relative ease with which they had seized power in Petrograd startled them. Natalia Sedova visited Smolny in the days following the coup. She found Lenin and Trotsky exhausted, "their faces . . . a grayish-green from lack of sleep; their eyes were inflamed, their collars soiled." Lenin and Trotsky tried to sleep on the floor, but their combined excitement and fatigue got the better of them. "'You know, from persecution and a life underground, to come so suddenly into power . . . ' Lenin whispered to Trotsky, his voice hesitating while he groped for the right phrase, settling on the German '*Es schwindelt*'—'It makes one dizzy.'"

With the Winter Palace in their hands, the Bolsheviks dominated the next session of the Congress. Under Lenin's leadership, it made three significant decisions. It endorsed a decree on peace, which appealed for a just settlement and called on the workers of France, Great Britain, and Germany to follow the lead of their Soviet brothers. It also endorsed a decree on land, which abolished the landed property of the gentry, the church, and the imperial family. The decree had originated among the Socialist Revolutionaries and by endorsing it, the Bolsheviks broadened their base of support among the peasants, who were now encouraged to take collective action and seize the large estates that had dominated the countryside.

Finally, the Congress declared the formation of a new government and a Central Executive Committee. Lenin became head of Sovnarkom (a new term for the Council of People's Commissars), while Trotsky was appointed commissar for foreign affairs. Lenin had initially suggested that Trotsky become head of the government out of deference to his role in the seizure of power. But Trotsky brushed the offer aside. Lenin's next idea for Trotsky was more difficult to resolve. Lenin urged him to accept the position of commissar of home affairs, from where he would direct actions against counterrevolution. Barely a day after the Bolsheviks took power, when the situation in the provinces was still uncertain, Trotsky believed that having a Jew in the role of chief enforcer would hand their enemies a useful tool. "Was it worthwhile to put into our enemies' hands such an additional weapon as my Jewish origin?" Trotsky asked. It was already enough of a shock that the autocracy and then the Provisional Government had both collapsed. He could not be oblivious to his Jewish origin and its likely effect, particularly among the peasants, where antisemitic attitudes remained widespread. Lenin had difficulty accepting the argument. "We are having a great international revolution," Lenin told him. "Of what importance are such trifles?" But Yakov Sverdlov, who was also Jewish (and would be named chairman of the Central Executive of the Soviets, in effect president of the country), concurred with Trotsky's reasoning. And it was Sverdlov who urged that Trotsky become commissar for foreign affairs, the second-most-important position after Lenin's.

Lenin and Trotsky formed the public face of the new regime. Any previous misgivings on Trotsky's part were behind him. Lenin was grateful for his newfound faith and, in a phrase that Trotsky often cited, Lenin declared "that from that time on, there has been no better Bolshevik."

They now faced overwhelming challenges. In the final days of October, Kerensky gathered several military units and attempted to storm Petrograd, but Trotsky, rallying soldiers and Red Guards, was able to repel the attack. In Moscow, the Bolsheviks engaged in heavy fighting for ten days before gaining control of the city. At the same time, the Mensheviks and Socialist Revolutionaries, joined by the powerful railway workers union, remained opposed to one-party rule. They attempted to negotiate with the Bolsheviks, hoping to broaden the government, even to see Lenin and Trotsky removed from the leadership. The negotiations led nowhere. Faced with such opposition, Lenin and Trotsky instituted repressive measures to consolidate control over the country. On October 27 the government issued its first decree, which authorized censorship of the press for the purpose of suppressing counterrevolution. To enforce it, the Bolsheviks dispatched teams to destroy printing presses, take away newsprint, and detain editors associated with opposition parties. As Lenin declared at the time, "Opposition newspapers were no less dangerous than bombs and machine guns." A month later, they ordered the arrest of leading Kadets, labeling it "a party of the enemies of the people." Then they detained Mensheviks, Right Socialist Revolutionaries, and peasant leaders; these were initial steps toward creating a police state. As the philosopher Nikolai Berdyaev commented in those years, "In Russian Communism the will for power is stronger than the will for liberty."

Such measures alarmed moderate Bolsheviks and other socialists, who did not hesitate to warn of a burgeoning political terror and the likelihood of civil war. Trotsky was not deterred. Committed to defending Bolshevik control, Lenin and Trotsky took whatever measures seemed necessary to hold on. "You wax indignant at the naked terror which we are applying against our class enemies," Trotsky declared, "but let me tell you that in one month's time at the most it will assume more frightful forms, modeled on the terror of the great French revolutionaries. Not the fortress but the guillotine will await our enemies."

Just two weeks after the revolution, Maxim Gorky saw enough of Bolshevik methods to issue a scathing judgment. "Lenin and Trotsky do not have the slightest idea of the meaning of freedom or the Rights of Man," he wrote in *Novaya*

Zhizn. "They have already become poisoned with the filthy venom of power, and this is shown by their shameful attitude toward freedom of speech, the individual, and all those other civil liberties for which the democracy struggled." A month later, the Bolsheviks created the Cheka—the secret police who would be known under different names, including the KGB—to sustain a monopoly of political power through the most frightful means of violence and intimidation. As Nikolai Sukhanov wrote that fall, the dictatorship of Lenin and Trotsky "rests on the bayonets of the soldiers and workers they deceived."

An even more fateful decision was soon to follow. After the tsar's abdication in February, all political parties declared support for a Constituent Assembly; it would be democratically elected and meet to decide the country's new form of government. Lenin and the Bolsheviks also endorsed this view. Elections for the Constituent Assembly took place in November and yielded a result that could only discomfit the Bolsheviks. The Socialist Revolutionaries (SRs) received 38 percent of the vote. (Their support was divided between Left SRs, who supported the Bolsheviks, and Right SRs, who did not; they had run on a single list, making it difficult to judge the ultimate meaning of the vote they received.)* The Bolsheviks received 24 percent, followed by much smaller ratios for the Mensheviks, the Kadets, and the Ukrainian SRs.

The vote was a major defeat for the Bolshevik regime. It immediately postponed convening the Constitutional Assembly, insisting that it could not take place until January 5. In the intervening weeks, Bolsheviks debated among themselves whether or not to permit the Assembly to meet; either way, Lenin would never allow a general election to annul the Bolsheviks' hold on power. The Assembly was scheduled to meet in Petrograd. The outcome could hardly surprise anyone. On that morning, tens

---

*A few weeks later, elections to the Soviet of Peasant Deputies gave an overwhelming majority to the Left Socialist Revolutionaries.

of thousands of supporters gathered outside the city and began to march toward the Tauride Palace. Without warning, Bolshevik marksmen fired on them, killing ten and wounding dozens of others.

With its anti-Bolshevik majority, the Constituent Assembly convened late that afternoon in an atmosphere of deep tension. Delegates debated for several hours, vainly trying to challenge the Bolshevik monopoly of power. When this one session adjourned in the early morning hours, the Bolsheviks made sure the Assembly would not reconvene. Any further hope for democratic reform in Russia was now dissolved. Trotsky fully supported the dispersal of the Constituent Assembly; in his eyes it would either obstruct the revolution or be superfluous to its success. Now only two things stood in the way: the German army on the borders of Russia and the gathering forces of armed opposition inside the country. Trotsky assumed responsibility to deter both.

Lenin's government set about dealing with the Germans. The decree on peace that Lenin had initiated in October was the basis for his strategy; it was part of his policy of revolutionary defeatism, which called upon workers to overthrow corrupt, bourgeois governments and bring an end to the war. Trotsky shared this belief in the prospects for revolution in Europe. Accepting the post of commissar for foreign affairs, he believed in his own presumptuous contention. As he told a friend at the time, "What diplomatic work are we apt to have? I will issue a few revolutionary proclamations to the peoples of the world, and then shut up shop." But things did not work out that way.*

On November 13 Trotsky offered the Germans both an

---

*During and after the revolution the French diplomat Louis de Robien was stationed in Petrograd, where he had several encounters with Trotsky. Watching him issue orders as foreign minister, de Robien believed that Trotsky was "lost in his dreams which to him are reality and on which he bases all his actions." See Louis de Robien, *The Diary of a Diplomat in Russia, 1917–1918* (New York, 1967), 174.

armistice and a willingness to discuss a general peace treaty. Within days, the Soviet delegation, which was headed by Trotsky's friend Adolph Yoffe and included Lev Kamenev, traveled to Brest Litovsk on the Polish border, where the German headquarters were located. Each side saw the advantage in agreeing to a separate peace. The Germans were hoping to transfer troops to the West, where they believed victory could be achieved over France and England. For Lenin, a separate peace would give Russia breathing room to recover from the upheavals of war and revolution; a general armistice might compel the Western powers to sue for peace as well. But as the talks wore on, the Germans grew impatient. They knew they had the upper hand if hostilities were to resume. To forestall a German advance, Lenin dispatched Trotsky to Brest Litovsk in the middle of December, hoping that his rhetorical powers could prolong the talks even further, giving revolution in Europe more time to burst forth. The Austrian foreign minister, Count Ottokar von Czernin, faced Trotsky across the table and recalled how impressive he could be. "Trotsky is undoubtedly an interesting, clever man and a very dangerous opponent. He has outstanding oratorical talent and an ability to make swift and effective retort as I have rarely seen, and with the insolence characteristic of his race." For Czernin, Trotsky was as much an irritating Jew as he was a defiant Bolshevik.

But events in Ukraine undercut Trotsky's plans. With German support, the Central Rada in Kiev (a kind of national congress), spurred on by Ukrainian nationalists, had declared independence for Ukraine at the end of November. Germany was in a position to make a separate peace with the Rada and occupy parts of Ukraine, further pressing the Bolsheviks. Then the Germans broadened their demands, insisting that Poland be detached from Russia and additional German gains be conceded in Lithuania and Latvia.

Trotsky quickly returned to Petrograd. Within Bolshevik ranks, three contending factions were emerging over how to deal with Germany. The most popular and extreme, led by Nikolai Bukharin, advocated resisting the German army in the name of revolution; he hoped to spark an upheaval in Berlin itself. Trotsky urged a different approach. Eager to extend the talks further, he put forward the clever slogan "Neither war nor peace." He proposed declaring a unilateral end to the war, while still refusing to sign a peace treaty that would recognize German territorial expansion. Only Lenin was willing to sue for an immediate peace, even if it meant losing precious territory. Safeguarding the revolution was all that mattered to Lenin. But he had yet to command a majority. So Lenin compromised, sided with Trotsky in order to avoid a suicidal war, and sent him back to Brest Litovsk.

But the Germans saw their chance. The kaiser ordered his negotiators to present an ultimatum to Trotsky: either sign an armistice or watch the German army advance. Trotsky was cornered but, still enamored of his rhetorical powers, declared that Russia would leave the war but refuse to accept German demands for more territory. Initially dumbfounded, German diplomats quickly recognized Russia's vulnerability: since there was no signed peace treaty, Germany was free to attack.

Within days, German armies quickly advanced, capturing Dvinsk in Latvia and Lutsk in Ukraine. With Petrograd vulnerable, the Bolsheviks moved the capital to Moscow, where Lenin and Trotsky soon took up quarters in the Kremlin, claiming the tsar's private rooms for their own. Lenin prevailed over his colleagues to sue for peace. He sent a telegram to Berlin accepting Germany's terms. It ceded so much territory to Germany and so many resources in agriculture and industry that no Soviet leader wanted to sign it, including Trotsky, who resigned as commissar for foreign affairs.* The treaty was signed

---

*Years later, Trotsky characterized the peace treaty as the "capitulation of a disarmed revolution before a powerful robber." See "Joseph Stalin," *Life*, October 2, 1939, p. 73.

by a lower-ranking Soviet diplomat on March 3. Trotsky's gambit succeeded only in allowing the Germans to seize more territory. It was Lenin who retained a more sober grasp of military and political reality. Despite the territorial sacrifice, he was willing to concede land in exchange for peace. The revolution would live on. But now outright civil war and foreign intervention by Russia's recent allies, as well as Japan, threatened all they had accomplished.

The Bolsheviks faced myriad enemies with guns. Former tsarist commanders assembled armies in Ukraine and in Siberia; in history they are referred to as the Whites. They were joined by nationalist forces who dreamed of independence for Ukraine, Georgia, and Armenia, as well as by Cossack units who wanted greater autonomy for their traditional homelands. No fewer than eighteen insurgent governments emerged by the summer of 1918, each determined to resist Bolshevik rule.

At the same time, foreign intervention deepened the crisis. Japanese troops landed in Vladivostok in early April. England, France, and the United States sent forces via the northern ports of Archangel and Murmansk, and to Odessa via the Black Sea. Deep inside Russia, a well-armed Czech legion of forty thousand men—made up of soldiers, students, and former prisoners of war—who had sided with Russia against the Central Powers was now making its way from the Volga through Siberia to Vladivostok, where it was planning to embark for the Western Front to fight Germany under French command. On their way across Russia, the Czechs assisted anti-Bolshevik movements, at times taking control of the Trans-Siberian Railway.

Of equal importance, by the spring and summer of 1918, the nature of Bolshevik rule was becoming increasingly apparent.* The Cheka was engaged in the arrest and murder of political opponents; peasants were angry over the confiscation of

*The Whites were also carrying out a brutal campaign of political murder.

grain; workers were expected to help revive industrial production and set aside hopes for independent trade unions. It was in this atmosphere, in March 1918, as the front was "taking more and more the shape of a noose closing ever tighter around Moscow," that Trotsky was appointed commissar of war and quickly assembled the Red Army.

His initiatives helped save the revolution. Without any military experience, Trotsky molded his forces into a regular army. It was his decision to mobilize the Red Guards who had defended the revolution in irregular, disorganized bands in cities and in factories. It was his decision to recruit thousands of tsarist officers; at one point, they made up three-fourths of the command structure of the Red Army. He then created a system of dual command by assigning a Bolshevik commissar to monitor them, and he turned the families of these officers into hostages to ensure their political loyalty. Kerensky had also employed commissars, but it was Trotsky who assigned them to every level of command and not only to those with the highest rank. And it was his decision to order mass conscription in the summer of 1918, bringing millions of peasants into the army.

Trotsky insisted on severe discipline to limit mutinies and desertions. In one episode in the small town of Svyazhsk, across the Volga from Kazan, Trotsky ordered the execution of a commander, a commissar, and nearly two dozen soldiers for desertion. "Cowards, scoundrels, and traitors will not escape bullets– this I pledge before the entire Red Army." There was no mistaking Trotsky's willingness to be ruthless. "To a gangrenous wound, a red-hot iron was applied" was how he described his decision in *My Life*. He was true to his word, ordering the execution of every tenth man in units refusing to fight.

It was Trotsky who was the principal witness against Admiral Alexei Shchastny, the commander of the Baltic Fleet, at his trial before the Supreme Revolutionary Tribunal on charges of sabotage and treason in June 1918; this was the first public trial to be employed as an instrument of Bolshevik terror. Shchastny was accused of leading a conspiracy to undermine Soviet control of the fleet. The admiral was not permitted to call defense witnesses and was executed within hours of the verdict, an unmistakable message to former tsarist officers to ensure their loyalty to the Bolshevik cause. Coming soon after the regime had voted to outlaw capital punishment, the case generated profound indignation among other socialist parties.

Nothing epitomized Trotsky's power and prestige more vividly than his armored train. Assembled in the late spring of 1918, the train allowed Trotsky to rush from one front to another—by some estimates, the train covered 125,000 miles during the Civil War—to assess the military challenge at hand, and to revive the morale of his troops. The train was so heavy that it needed to be pulled by two engines. It initially included a printing press, a telegraph station, a radio and electric power station, a restaurant, a library, a garage, and a bath. His personal office offered leather armchairs, a sofa, wall maps, and typewriters nailed down to his secretaries' desks. Later, when the train was divided into two, Trotsky added an aviation unit with two small airplanes, several automobiles, and a band. Anxious about possible ambushes, Trotsky was also heavily protected; a dozen bodyguards accompanied him on the train, while a small unit of soldiers invariably surrounded him when he visited the front.

Journalists were often on board, and Trotsky used their presence to convey an image of being the all-powerful military commander; he even took to wearing a leather jacket of his own design to underscore his brutal efficiency. (This uniform became the distinctive garb of the Cheka's commissars.) One of the journalists was Larisa Reisner, who was with him in Svyazhsk. They were lovers at the time. In *My Life*, Trotsky paid tribute to her talent and her beauty: "She flashed across the revolutionary sky like a burning meteor, blinding many.

With her appearance of an Olympian goddess, she combined a subtle and ironical mind and the courage of a warrior." Reisner survived the Civil War only to succumb to typhus in Moscow in 1926.

The fighting that broke out in 1918 covered wide areas of Russia and Ukraine. Like all civil wars, the violence was cruel and indiscriminate. The Whites' cause proved to be hopeless. White armies, led by various tsarist commanders, failed to coordinate their movements across Russia's vast territory, giving the Red Army time to exploit interior lines of communication. The Whites could not accept the collapse of the autocracy or arouse enough popular support in a country where the vast majority understood that Russia could not revert back to a monarchy or resume the fight against the Central Powers. They were defending a shameful, moribund regime and this decided their fate.

At times, nonetheless, the Whites posed a serious challenge. General Anton Denikin seized control of Kiev and large parts of Ukraine more than once, and the fighting there was often accompanied by fierce pogroms, leaving up to 150,000 Jews dead at the hands of Ukrainian nationalists and White armies. Operating in Siberia and the Urals, the Czech Legion and Admiral Alexander Kolchak threatened Yekaterinburg, where the tsar was being held in July 1918. Earlier that month, Lenin and the Politburo had approved of the tsar's execution in principle. But when the Czech Legion surrounded the city in mid-July, Lenin persuaded other Bolshevik leaders, in particular Yakov Sverdlov, to order the execution of Tsar Nicholas II, Tsarina Alexandra, their children, and their servants. The Bolsheviks had to ensure that no one would succeed in rescuing the Romanovs and then use the tsar to unify opposition to Bolshevik rule. (The Czechs captured the city eight days after the execution.) Trotsky's role in the executions is not entirely clear—he claimed that he learned about their fate only shortly after the murders. He had dreamed of bringing the tsar to trial for his crimes and assuming for himself the role of chief prosecutor.

The following year, in the spring of 1919, the Bolsheviks faced their gravest threat. White units drew near to Moscow and Petrograd. Lenin was so unnerved that he considered abandoning the defense of the former imperial capital. But Trotsky insisted on going to Petrograd himself and personally led his men on horseback as they threw the Whites back.

For a time, Trotsky's prestige was unassailable. Bertrand Russell visited Moscow in the spring of 1920. He saw Trotsky at the Bolshoi Opera and came away impressed "with his good looks, lightning intelligence and magnetic personality." For Russell, Trotsky had "the vanity of an artist or actor," particularly when he acknowledged the cheers of the audience. Trotsky also charmed another British visitor, the sculptor Clare Sheridan, who was a first cousin to Winston Churchill. Sympathetic to the Bolsheviks, she came to Russia in the fall of 1920 to work on portrait busts of leading party figures, including Lenin and Trotsky. It seems likely that she had an affair with Trotsky. "He is a charming personality with a keen forceful sensitive face and a particularly delightful voice," she wrote about him. "We have discussed everything from Shakespeare, Shelley & Sheridan to international politics, to mutual personalities! He has the subtle mind of a Latin, who can convey anything without actually expressing it. His talk is full of imagination and imagery. Of course this place has spoilt one for brains, everyone is so brilliant, but Trotsky is perhaps the most delightful to talk to that I have met yet."

In *My Life*, Trotsky took pride in quoting a Cossack who had served in the Red Army. A White Guard writer had related how this Cossack faced taunts because of his service "under the Jew—Trotsky." The Cossack quickly retorted, "Nothing of the sort. Trotsky is not a Jew, Trotsky is a fighter. He's ours . . . Russian!" the Cossack insisted. "It is Lenin who is a Communist, a Jew." Even Stalin acknowledged Trotsky's importance. Writing in *Pravda* on the first anniversary of the revolution, Stalin credited Trotsky for carrying out "all the work of practical organization of the insurrection. . . . It may be said with certainty that the bold execution of the work of the Military Revolutionary Committee, the party owes principally and above all to Comrade Trotsky." Fine words in 1918. Anyone who dared to echo such a compliment not so many years later was subjected to exile, imprisonment, or worse.

Nonetheless, in spite of his military successes, there were party leaders who questioned Trotsky's judgment, particularly over the enlistment of tsarist officers and the army's harsh discipline and authoritarian chain of command. Faced with serious challenges to his leadership, Trotsky offered to resign as commissar of war, but Lenin refused to accept his resignation and offered Trotsky blanket authorization to carry on. "Show me another man able to organize almost a model army within a single year and win the respect of military experts," Lenin told Gorky. "We have such a man. We have everything. And we shall work wonders."

During the Civil War, Trotsky also had to deal with antisemitic attitudes among the population. He voiced his concern over the high number of Jews in the Cheka, knowing that their presence could only provoke hatred toward Jews as a group. He successfully recruited Jews for the Red Army because they were eager to avenge pogrom attacks, but argued in vain in favor of forming Jewish units, hoping that they would counteract antisemitic claims that Jews were avoiding military service. On at least one occasion, in July 1920, he heard about a unit of Red Guards that was targeting Jews in Novorossiysk; his intervention brought an end to the pogrom.

At the same time, newspapers circulating in White-held territory used the image of Trotsky to stir opposition against the Bolsheviks. Followers of Simon Petlyura in Ukraine were known to scream "Down with Trotsky" during their murderous attacks on Jewish towns.* Black Hundred leaflets claimed that Trotsky was turning churches into movie theaters but leaving synagogues alone. Another leaflet claimed that Lenin and Trotsky wanted to convert all the peasants into Jews and then circumcise them, while yet another described how the Jews were the carriers of Bolshevism, as if Bolshevism had infected their blood. In a country where Jews had been persecuted and marginalized for so long, it must have been unnerving for millions of people to see Jews among those in charge of the country.

At one point a delegation of Jews arranged to meet General Denikin, intending to plead for an end to the pogroms. Ordinary Jews, they told him, should not be held responsible for Trotsky any more than ordinary Russians should be held accountable for Lenin. But it was too convenient for Whites and antisemites to subscribe to such logic, at least when it came to the Jews.

Trotsky could be eloquent in the face of pogroms but still express disdain for Jews' parochial interests. He had no desire, for example, to protect Jewish religious institutions. He could neither identify nor sympathize with the sensibilities that lay behind them; he had none of his own.

Trotsky lacked *ahavat yisroel*—a love for the Jewish people —or a commitment to its historical continuity. The Jews were just another small, persecuted minority. As a child he did not

---

*Simon Petlyura (1879–1926) was a Ukrainian nationalist and opponent of the Bolsheviks who has long been accused of directing murderous pogroms against Jewish communities in Ukraine during the Russian Civil War. He was assassinated in Paris on May 25, 1926.

identify with his fellow Jews. As an adolescent in Odessa, he lived with a self-identified Jewish family but absorbed little if any emotional attachment to his origin. When the allure of Marxism captured his imagination and his faith, Trotsky abandoned his Jewish identity. For him, it was a necessary step toward embracing all of humanity (or at least the proletariat). So he claimed that prejudice against the Jews was not a major factor in his hatred of the autocracy. So he could assert he was a Marxist and a Russian revolutionary, then deny his identity as a Jew. But his rejection of his Jewish origin was itself a form of engagement. As he spurned one messianic religion, he adopted an alternative utopian faith—one that was secular and far more dangerous.

Trotsky spent a good deal of his adult life among Jews—in London, Paris, Vienna, New York, and Russia itself; his strategy, deliberate or unconscious, must have been relentless in order to withstand nostalgic attraction. Sitting in the Kremlin during and after the Civil War, he turned away delegations of Jewish communal and religious leaders who thought he might be open to special appeals. When Rabbi Jacob Mase of Moscow came to him for assistance, Trotsky declared: "I am not a Jew. I'm a Marxist internationalist. . . . I have nothing in common with Jewish things and want to know nothing about Jewish things." In Trotsky's eyes, the Jewish petitioners were assuming an intimate connection that he refused to affirm. So he turned away appeals from observant Jews; they were an unwelcome reminder of his origin, a piece of his identity he thought he had left behind, as if he could resign from the Jewish people. After their meeting, Rabbi Mase was reported to observe, "The Trotskys make the revolutions, and the Bronsteins pay the bills." (Zinoviev claimed that in 1918 rabbis in Odessa excommunicated him and Trotsky.) Trotsky was neither ashamed of his Jewish origin nor ashamed to deny them. On party forms he wrote in "Jew" as his nationality. When he arrived in Mexico in January 1937, he wrote the word *nothing* in the blank on his Mexican passport for religious affiliation.*

As the Bolsheviks consolidated their hold on Russia, their repressive measures unsettled many onetime allies in Western Europe, Rosa Luxemburg and Karl Kautsky among them. Luxemburg and Trotsky had once shared a loathing for Lenin's insistence on a disciplined, centralized party. Now, in 1918, she understood where Lenin's tactics were taking Russia. "Without general elections," she wrote, "without unrestricted freedom of press and assembly, without a free struggle of opinion, life dies out in every public institution, becomes a mere semblance of life, in which only the bureaucracy remains as the active element. . . . Public life gradually disappears; a few dozen extremely energetic and highly idealistic party leaders rule. . . . Au fond this is the rule of a clique—a dictatorship it is true, but not the dictatorship of the proletariat, but of a handful of politicians."

Karl Kautsky weighed in as well. In 1918 and 1919 he published two pamphlets, *The Dictatorship of the Proletariat* and *Terrorism and Communism.* Writing as a veteran socialist, Kautsky held onto his belief in democracy. He derided Lenin's dictatorship as nothing more than a monopoly of power by a single political party. Without the support of a majority of the people, who had the right to express their political will, no political movement could impose socialism on an unwilling population. The attempt could only lead to an outright dictatorship, which would have to rely on force and intimidation—terror—to sustain its hold on power and bend society to its will.

Kautsky struck a nerve. Both Lenin and Trotsky responded

*In the Soviet Union, the Jews were recognized as a separate nationality, so it was not altogether inconsistent for Trotsky to acknowledge himself as a Jew by nationality at the same time that he denied having any religious identification.

with pamphlets of their own. Trotsky did not flinch. In *Terrorism and Communism* (a title he copied from Kautsky), Trotsky did more than defend the use of force during a civil war; he argued that such methods were necessary for the creation of socialism. "Who aims at the end cannot reject the means," he argued. Yes, the Reds and the Whites both engaged in violence to achieve their goals, but what the Bolsheviks had in mind was so fundamentally aimed at benefiting *everyone* that their use of coercion should be justified, while similar methods on the part of reactionaries, who were serving only a relative few, deserved to be condemned. The integrity of motives was all that mattered. "A revolution," he declared, "is not decided by votes. . . . Repression [is] the necessary means of breaking the will of the opposing side." Trotsky never repudiated these ideas even in embattled opposition when he became the principal target of Stalin's wrath.

There was no mistaking Trotsky's radical urges. This was the crux of the tragedy, for Trotsky personally and more significantly for Russia itself. The country was now in the hands of determined Marxists who would stop at nothing to hold onto power and impose their ideological views. In *Terrorism and Communism*, Trotsky argued that whatever the party decided could only be interpreted as motivated solely by its commitment to advancing the cause of the working class. With the revolution, everything was possible. To defend the revolution, nothing was forbidden.

Terrorism, too, could be employed in the name of the revolution. "Intimidation is a powerful weapon of policy," Trotsky wrote from his armored train in 1920. "War, like revolution, is founded upon intimidation. A victorious war, generally speaking, destroys only an insignificant part of the conquered army, intimidating the remainder and breaking their will. The revolution works in the same way: it kills individuals, and intimidates thousands." Censorship, summary executions, torture, political imprisonment, and exile—all were justified in the name of building socialism.

There had been a time when Trotsky mistrusted Lenin's methods, when he understood that the insistence on control would inevitably lead to dictatorship and ruin. But now he had tasted power. Like Lenin, Trotsky could be indifferent to human suffering if it was being inflicted in the name of his Marxist faith. Angela Balabanoff was a longtime friend. Seeing this transformation, she could not help but observe that Trotsky "was a neophyte who wanted to outdo in zeal and ardor the Bolsheviks themselves, the neophyte who wanted to be forgiven the many crimes against Bolshevism he had committed in the past—by becoming more intransigent, more revolutionary, more Bolshevik than any of them." Now the thirst to hold onto power led Bolshevik leaders into a cruel and murderous world that would consume many of them, not least of all Trotsky himself.

The Civil War was over by the spring of 1921. But unrest over Bolshevik methods roiled the country. Famine, strikes by urban workers, and peasant revolts challenged Lenin's regime. The economy was in shambles, undermined by years of war and revolution, by forced expropriations of grain to feed the cities, and by Bolshevik experiments involving the use of barter and the suspension of money. Trotsky did not emerge from the civil war with the popularity he no doubt expected.* The same qualities that contributed to his effectiveness as commissar of war undermined his popularity within the party. Through the

---

*In December 1919 the small town of Ivashchenkovo near Samara was renamed Trotsk in his honor, and in 1923 the town of Gatchina near Petrograd was also renamed Trotsk. Before that, only Lenin had been so celebrated; several small towns and villages were renamed in his honor during his lifetime; Petrograd became Leningrad in 1924 only after Lenin's death. No town was renamed for Stalin until March 1924, when Yuzovka in the Donbass became Stalin, and then sometime later Stalino. It was renamed Donetsk in 1957 four years after Stalin's death. Tsaritsyn was renamed Stalingrad in April 1925.

force of his intellect and eloquence, Trotsky commanded authority whenever he addressed a crowd. It also gave him the appearance of a demagogue. Now there was resentment over his authoritarian methods, his personal vanity, his often abrupt, arrogant manner, his clashes with other party leaders such as Stalin over military strategy. Bolsheviks looked to the French Revolution as a guide to their own. Ever mindful of Napoleon's role, they worried that Trotsky might exploit his military prestige to stage a coup. Trotsky had only recently joined the Bolsheviks; in their eyes, his attachment to the state or the army seemed stronger than his ties to the party. On paper Trotsky remained commissar of war, but with the Civil War over, his power as a political leader began to fade.

Trotsky turned his attention to the economy with the sort of authoritarian approach he had used in the Red Army. He urged the creation of labor battalions, which would assign demobilized soldiers to specific tasks in industry and agriculture. He argued against granting trade unions any degree of autonomy, convinced that under communism workers would not need to improve their conditions or defend their rights. Workers and factory managers shared the goal of increasing productivity, where all would benefit equally. In March 1920 Trotsky was appointed commissar of transport, responsible for overseeing the railways. Here, too, he relied on harsh central planning, draconian measures to counter absenteeism, and an insistence that workers be prepared to sacrifice special Saturdays and Sundays for unpaid assignments.

Trotsky's ideas generated protests among the workers. The Menshevik leader Raphael Abramovich came to their defense. Speaking at a trade union congress in Moscow, he likened Trotsky's militarization of labor to the Pharoahs' methods of building the pyramids. In response, Trotsky reverted to a doctrinaire formula, asserting that Abramovich was oblivious to the class nature of government. "Our compulsion," Trotsky reminded him, "is applied by a workers' and peasants' government." Such rhetoric antagonized even other Bolsheviks, like Mikhail Tomsky and Grigory Zinoviev, who argued in favor of allowing trade unions to defend workers' rights. Lenin weighed in on the side of Trotsky's critics, concerned that Trotsky's approach and his strident criticism of other party leaders was undermining party unity.

A more serious crisis soon challenged the party. The Kronstadt sailors were increasingly angry over the growing dictatorship and the plight of the peasants; secure in their fortified island bastion, they staged a mutiny and called for democratic rights. In a defiant proclamation, they denounced the October Revolution for enslaving the Russian people.

> The power of the monarchy, with its police and its gendarmerie, has passed into the hands of the Communist usurpers, who have given the people not freedom but the constant fear of torture by the Cheka. . . . To the protests of the peasants, expressed in spontaneous uprisings, and those of the workers, whose living conditions have compelled them to strike, they have answered with mass executions and a bloodletting that exceeds even the tsarist generals.

Their appeal was supported by Socialist Revolutionaries inside the country and by émigré communities in Europe. The regime feared a renewal of the Civil War. Lenin and Trotsky could not acknowledge the legitimacy of the sailors' criticism. Instead, they denounced it as inspired by "French counterintelligence" and "SR–Black Hundred" thinking. Trotsky was dispatched to Petrograd to lead the counterattack. He immediately called for the rebels to surrender or face the Red Army. When his ultimatum was ignored, he sent a large force to cross the frozen Gulf of Finland and storm the fortress, but the sailors, manning artillery and naval guns, shot out large holes in the ice, causing the troops, who were trying to advance during a blinding snowstorm, to fall in and drown by the hundreds.

The Red Army regrouped. On March 16, determined to storm Kronstadt before the spring thaw made the fortress invincible, a much larger force of fifty thousand troops crossed the open ice. This time they succeeded. The rebellion was suppressed. The surviving sailors were paraded through the streets of Petrograd. Two thousand were subsequently executed; others succumbed to a more agonizing death in the new concentration camp in Solovki on an island in the White Sea.

Trotsky's role in the Kronstadt Rebellion haunted his life and reputation. There was no mistaking his willingness to kill to preserve the revolution. He and Lenin had engaged in a deliberate distortion of the rebels' motives to justify harsh suppression, claims Trotsky repeated in the years that followed. Once in exile, Trotsky did his best to avoid discussing the episode. He even denied participating in the assault on the fortress or in the reprisals that followed, while his followers, anxious to clear his name of any cloud, denied his involvement after his death. No one connected to Trotsky was interested in the truth. Trotsky hardly mentioned it in his memoirs and devoted a single sentence to Kronstadt in his book on Stalin, dismissing the sailors as "a few dubious Anarchists and SRs" who "were sponsoring a handful of revolutionary peasants and soldiers in rebellion."

The Kronstadt episode took place during the Tenth Party Congress. Faced by multiple revolts among workers, peasants, and sailors, Lenin took two major steps. Knowing that he needed to repudiate War Communism and revive the economy, Lenin initiated the New Economic Policy (NEP), a set of reforms that permitted the return of capitalist methods. Lenin also faced challenges from factions within the party: a Workers' Opposition, led by Alexandra Kollontai, objected to privileges the party had granted itself and called for greater democracy—within both the party and society at large. Kollontai and her allies sought to take on the bureaucratic elite that was increasingly running the country. Lenin would have none of this.

He argued for an end to factions within the party, making it illegal to organize opposition to official policies. His proposal passed with an overwhelming majority, a fateful development to which Trotsky lent his support. This decision not only undermined free discussion within the party but also led to the creation of the post of general secretary, whose job was to enforce party discipline and recruit new, loyal members. Lenin appointed Joseph Stalin to this position in April 1922. Stalin was little known at the time. Within a year, he used his post to guarantee his own control of the party.

At times Trotsky also went along with severe repression of cultural life. During the summer of 1922 he endorsed the forced exile of more than two hundred leading intellectuals, who were branded as counterrevolutionaries and sent out of the country on two ships. Lenin had been planning this move for several months; the Bolsheviks were growing increasingly concerned over the example of poets, writers, and philosophers voicing their ideas about individual freedom and publishing independent journals, particularly in Petrograd. Infused with a sense of Christian humanism, individual thinkers like Nikolai Berdyaev and Semyon Frank were trying to imagine an alternative way forward for the country somewhere between the extremes of Russian autocracy and Bolshevik ideology. For the Bolsheviks, though, there could be no tolerance for such subversive ideas. As Trotsky explained in an interview with the American journalist Louise Bryant, "Those elements whom we are sending or will send [abroad] are politically worthless in themselves. But they are potential weapons in the hands of our possible enemies. In the event of new military complications, . . . all these unreconciled and incorrigible elements will turn into military-political elements of the enemy. And we will be forced to shoot them." For Trotsky, these intellectuals were nothing more than a Fifth Column. But he encouraged Bryant to see their expulsion as an act of mercy and to defend the Bolsheviks in the Western press.

In reality, the Bolsheviks understood and feared the values these intellectuals represented. Lenin and Trotsky had emerged from the same social and cultural milieu, but their extreme utopian vision separated them from others who retained a commitment to individual creativity and intellectual dissent; such values had animated opposition to the tsar, and Lenin and Trotsky could not allow this competing set of values to get in the way of the Bolsheviks' dehumanizing dogmas. Their extreme ideology was a betrayal of the moral tradition from which they had emerged.

Although Trotsky was a genuinely sophisticated student of literature, he was not above engaging in shallow Marxist criticism. In 1922 hard-line Marxist critics were training their sights on the poet Anna Akhmatova. She was recognized as one of the country's most accomplished poets; even *Pravda* carried a sympathetic article about her, although her verse had no political content and conjured a world of private emotion. Trotsky weighed into the controversy. In his collection *Literature and Revolution*, he took aim at both Akhmatova and Marina Tsvetaeva, another poet whose verses had gained literary acclaim:

> One reads with dismay most of the poetic collections, especially those of the women. Here, indeed, one cannot take a step without God. The lyric circle of Akhmatova and Tsvetaeva ... is very small. He [God] is a very convenient and portable third person, quite domestic, a friend of the family who fulfills from time to time the duties of a doctor of female ailments. How this individual, no longer young, burdened with the personal and too often bothersome errands of Akhmatova, Tsvetaeva, and others, can manage in his spare time to direct the destinies of the universe, is simply incomprehensible.

To give Trotsky his due, he at least in theory advocated a nondoctrinaire approach to censorship. As he wrote in *Literature and Revolution*, "Art cannot live and cannot develop without a flexible atmosphere of sympathy around it." And in this volume's most widely quoted paragraph, he counseled patience:

> Art must make its own way and by its own means. The methods of Marxism are not the same as those of art. The party leads the proletariat but not the processes of history. There are domains in which the party leads, directly and commandingly. There are domains in which it only cooperates. There are domains, finally, in which it orientates itself. The domain of art is not one in which the party is called upon to command.

Nonetheless, for Trotsky political considerations could still override artistic sensibilities. No art that opposed the revolution could be tolerated, a principle that different censors interpreted according to different standards. For Trotsky this meant "a watchful revolutionary censorship . . . free from petty, partisan maliciousness," but censorship nonetheless.

Literature and Revolution is also famous for the expression of Trotsky's utopian vision of cultural life under Communism.

> All the arts—literature, drama, painting, music and architecture—will lend this process beautiful form. More correctly, the shell in which the cultural construction and self-education of Communist man will be enclosed will develop all the vital elements of contemporary art to the highest point. Man will become immeasurably stronger, wiser, and subtler; his body will become more harmonized, his movements more rhythmic, his voice more musical. The forms of life will become dynamically dramatic. The average human type will rise to the heights of an Aristotle, a Goethe, or a Marx. And above this ridge new peaks will rise.*

In 1923, as Stalin was amassing greater influence, Trotsky continued to write on a host of topics. The country was benefiting from the more relaxed atmosphere brought on by the

---

*For a time, the young Saul Bellow was particularly drawn to Trotsky's views on culture. "He had me fooled," Bellow once wrote a friend. "Alas for poor him, and poor us."

New Economic Policy. Trotsky and other Bolshevik leaders believed it was time to highlight the need for cultural and social reforms, alongside the country's political transformation. In his collection of essays *Problems of Everyday Life*, Trotsky explored the challenge of social equality for women at a time when family relations were breaking down. In a postrevolutionary society, it was time to repair the country's infrastructure, broaden literacy, "reduce the cost of production of shoes in Soviet factories, combat filth, catch swindlers, extend power cables into the countryside." His ideas provoked discussion and controversy, but looking back on 1923, when Lenin was slowly dying and Stalin was grasping the reins of power, Trotsky was scribbling away about secondary problems while the fate of the country and his own personal destiny were being decided.

After so many years of violent rhetoric against Lenin, Trotsky was now prepared to heap praise on him. His admiration was genuine. On April 23, 1920, when Lenin turned fifty, Trotsky wrote a tribute for the front page of *Pravda*. His pompous language carried intimations of the cult that later surrounded Lenin's name:

> A clear scientific system—materialistic dialectics—is necessary for action on the historical scale that fell on Lenin's shoulders. Necessary but not sufficient. Here a hidden creative force is also needed, which we call intuition: the ability to quickly evaluate events, to separate the essential and important from the husks and the trifles, to imaginatively fill in missing pieces of a picture, to second-guess others, especially your enemies, and to combine all this together and strike a blow as soon as the "formula" for the blow takes shape in your mind. This is the intuition of action. His scientific works were only preparation for action. If he had not published even one book in the past, he would have entered history as he is entering it today: as the leader of the proletarian revolution, the founder of the Third International.

But the party had a long memory; past disputes were not permitted to fade away. A curious incident in December 1921 underscored Trotsky's growing vulnerability.

Historians of the party came across documents from Trotsky's old polemics with the Bolsheviks, including vicious denunciations of Lenin. One letter in particular, which Trotsky had sent to Nikolai Chkheidze in 1913, referred to Lenin as an "intriguer," a "disorganizer," and "an exploiter of Russian backwardness." In deference to Trotsky, a party archivist named Mikhail Olminsky asked him whether the material could be published. In his written response, Trotsky advised against publication, explaining that it was pointless to dwell on old and forgotten disputes. The material was held back from the public, but it still circulated quietly, a vivid reminder to Old Bolsheviks that not so long before Trotsky had been an outspoken critic of Lenin. As Stalin recruited new members who could not appreciate how Social Democrats had once debated among themselves, the image of Trotsky as an outsider, as someone who had repeatedly denounced Lenin, undermined his image within ever-growing circles in the party.

Trotsky did not realize how much his own standing depended on Lenin's health. Lenin was only fifty-two when he had his first stroke in May 1922. Initially, it left him paralyzed on his right side. Trotsky did not even learn of Lenin's illness for three days, until Bukharin sought him out to inform him. "This could have been no accident," Trotsky wrote years later. "Those who for a long time had been preparing to become my opponents—Stalin above all—were anxious to gain time." After months of convalescence, Lenin gradually recovered some strength only to suffer more strokes. Stalin, in his role as general secretary, controlled access to Lenin and monitored his medical care. Lenin also confided in him, at times suggesting that Stalin give him poison to avoid a long-term debilitating illness. Joined by Kamenev and Zinoviev, Stalin looked for ways to gain advantage, to prepare for Lenin's demise, and to forestall Trotsky's coming to power.

Trotsky was curiously passive as Stalin deepened his influence within the party, unmindful that others were already engaged in a struggle over succession. Lenin's private attitude toward Trotsky and Stalin remains disputed among historians. Certainly there were times when Lenin favored Trotsky, perhaps to promote him as a preferred successor. In April 1922, for example, Lenin nominated Trotsky to be deputy chairman of the Council of People's Commissars. (Stalin had become general secretary of the party a week earlier.) But Trotsky turned him down, convinced that such a position, with little authority of its own and overlapping with both government and party officials, afforded him little substantial influence. As he said at the time, "Every commissar is doing too many jobs and every job was done by too many commissars." The bureaucracy was growing too large, leaving Trotsky increasingly marginalized. Lenin repeated the offer several times that year, but each time Trotsky refused. Was Lenin hoping to balance the evident authority of the party by appointing Trotsky to lead the government? Perhaps. But with the end of the Civil War, Trotsky did not assume another official position that matched the prestige or power that he had once enjoyed. He was among the country's leading literary critics. He lectured on economics. He had a productive influence on the course of Soviet Russia's initial diplomatic successes, helping to forge political and military ties to Germany and revive fruitful negotiations with Great Britain. In the eyes of the public, the country continued to be led by Lenin and Trotsky. Stalin himself later acknowledged that after Lenin, Trotsky was the most popular figure in the country.

But the ground was shifting under his feet. As soon as Stalin became general secretary, he began maneuvering to succeed Lenin. Always, his eye was on Trotsky. But Trotsky was not driven to seek power. Supporters might regard this as a mark of integrity, an indication that he did not harbor Bonapartist pretensions. But it could also be seen as a type of arrogance, as a reflection of Trotsky's presumption that his stature as a revolutionary and military leader ensured that when the time came, he would be recognized as Lenin's inevitable successor. He was prepared to accept power; he was not prepared to campaign for it. This left him ill equipped for the ensuing struggle. There was a tragic gap between Trotsky's strategic brilliance in 1905 and 1917 and his strategic and tactical blunders during the many months of Lenin's illness. At every turn, even when advantages favored him, he acted with little sense of purpose. Each misstep left him more vulnerable than before. Writing in his memoirs years later, Trotsky sought to explain his lack of resolve. "Independent action on my part would have been interpreted, or to be more exact, represented as my personal fight for Lenin's place in the party and state. The very thought of this made me shudder." But more was at stake than Trotsky's place in history. He knew Stalin well enough to understand that the fate of the revolution was in jeopardy. But he failed to muster sufficient resolve to defend it.

Trotsky also was mesmerized by his understanding of Marxism. It was social forces—the masses—that determined the fate of revolutions. Stalin was not interested in such theories; he wanted his hands on the levers of power. That meant taking discreet control of the party apparatus and then using it to his advantage when the time came.* Stalin's strategy did not conform to Trotsky's theory of power. It is an irony of history that in 1917, in spite of his intellectual commitment to an orthodox, Marxist theory of revolution, Trotsky organized the

*As Trotsky recognized near the end of his life, Stalin's strategy marked "a unique case in world history: Stalin succeeded in concentrating dictatorial power in his hands before one percent of the population knew his name!"

seizure of bridges and government institutions because that was how to gain control of Petrograd. But when Stalin was seizing control of the party, Trotsky did not realize what was happening until it was too late. He seemed to be helpless. It is a terrible, almost unfathomable irony of his life that one whose name and presence shook the rafters of chancelleries proved politically naive and vulnerable before Stalin's maneuverings. No less a figure than Milovan Djilas, the famous Yugoslav dissident Marxist, made his own harsh assessment of Trotsky's fundamental weakness as a politician: "Trotsky, an excellent speaker, brilliant stylist, and skilled polemicist, a man cultured and of excellent intelligence, was deficient in only one quality: a sense of reality." In Trotsky's case, his blindness to what was unfolding around him contained an element of self-deception and contributed to his downfall.

Lenin's attitude toward both men was still evolving over the winter of 1922–1923. With his strength dwindling, Lenin grew increasingly concerned about the succession. In December he began to compose his political testament. Written as a letter to the next party congress, it reviewed likely successors—veteran Bolsheviks like Zinoviev and Kamenev, Yury Pyatakov and Bukharin, alongside both Stalin and Trotsky—and found each to be wanting in some degree. Sensing that Trotsky and Stalin would probably lead opposing sides in any significant political dispute, Lenin appeared reluctant to express a preference for either, hoping to avoid a major split within the party.

> Comrade Stalin, having become general secretary, has concentrated unlimited power in his hands, and I am not convinced that he will always manage to use this power with sufficient care. On the other hand, Comrade Trotsky . . . is characterized not only by outstanding talents. To be sure he is personally the most capable person in the present Central Committee, but he also overbrims with self-confidence and

with an excessive preoccupation with the purely administrative side of things.

Unbeknownst to Lenin, one of his secretaries shared a copy with Stalin, who ordered her to destroy it. But copies remained in Lenin's safe.

Within ten days, Lenin felt the need to reconsider. He added an additional paragraph, this time targeting Stalin specifically and calling for his ouster:

> Stalin is too crude, and this defect, which is entirely acceptable in our milieu and in relationships among us as Communists, become unacceptable in the position of general secretary. I therefore propose to comrades that they should devise a means of removing him from this job and should appoint to this job someone else who is distinguished from comrade Stalin in all other respects only by the single superior aspect that he should be more tolerant, more polite and more attentive toward comrades, less capricious, etc.

Lenin had made up his mind. Anxious to curb Stalin's authority, Lenin summoned Trotsky and encouraged him to challenge Stalin at the XIIth Party Congress over his authoritarian methods in Georgia. Soviet Russia had conquered Georgia in 1921, wresting control from a popular Menshevik government. But then Stalin went a step further, purging a group of Georgian Bolsheviks with such arbitrary methods that even Lenin took offense. Stalin, moreover, was proposing to centralize the national government's authority to such an extent that the *new* Union of Soviet Socialist Republics began to resemble the *old* administrative structure of tsarist Russia—the prison of the peoples—by refusing to recognize the rights of small nationalities.

Lenin was now suspicious of Stalin's character and angry over Stalin's personal insult to his wife, Nadezhda Krupskaya, when she was gathering material about events in Georgia.

Lenin had prepared a letter to Stalin threatening to "break off all personal relations." In retrospect, this was a potential hinge moment; the subsequent history of the Soviet Union could have moved in a different direction. But Trotsky failed to take on Stalin as Lenin wished him to. Satisfied that he and Lenin were in agreement and that Stalin would accept whatever terms he proposed, Trotsky merely asked Stalin to reword the text of his speech before the congress, verbally mollify the Georgians, and express opposition to Great Russian chauvinism. His generosity toward Stalin went further. Trotsky controlled Lenin's notes about the Georgian affair and by sharing them with the party could have undermined Stalin's claim on the succession. But here again, Trotsky failed to press his advantage and left it with the Politburo to decide what to do. Neither Lenin's personal letter to Stalin nor his notes about Georgia became known to the broader party until Nikita Khrushchev denounced Stalin in 1956. Lenin had warned Trotsky not to accept a "rotten compromise" regardless of how Stalin might beseech him. But that was exactly what Trotsky did. As for the political testament, it was read to selected party leaders but not shared with all the delegates; any damage to Stalin was limited.

Trotsky's curious pattern of passivity has long provoked debate among observers of his career. Even Trotsky's close friend Adolph Yoffe rebuked Trotsky for his diffidence when the situation demanded an aggressive striving for power—one that would match Stalin's own. Yoffe committed suicide in 1927, in part out of despair over Trotsky's expulsion from the party. In his suicide note, Yoffe wrote to Trotsky, "I have always believed that you lacked Lenin's *unbending will, his unwillingness to yield.*" As Yoffe witnessed, Trotsky had held back.

But he did not hold back entirely. In the fall of 1923 Trotsky and dozens of his followers, calling themselves the Left Opposition, tried to mount a challenge against Kamenev, Zinoviev, and Stalin. In a letter by Trotsky and in a subsequent declaration signed by forty-six leading party figures, they called for greater democracy within the party, a reversal of the party's severe bureaucratization, and more radical economic reforms. Trotsky was even able to elaborate his views in *Pravda* that December in the vain hope of overcoming his opponents' growing ascendancy. But he was running out of options and out of time.

Lenin died on January 21, 1924. This was a Monday. Trotsky was traveling south to Sukhumi, hoping to recover from a recurrent fever that had ravished him for three months, ever since he had hunted for ducks in a cold bog. Stalin informed Trotsky of Lenin's death and also confirmed that the funeral would take place on Saturday, making it impossible for Trotsky to return to Moscow in time. Trotsky felt no political urgency to rush back and did not "attribute transcendental importance" to being present. He refused to request extraordinary measures: to dispatch a special train, to clear the tracks of snow in the north. In fact, the funeral did not take place until Sunday, a day later, meaning that it would have been possible for Trotsky to attend. He was in Sukhumi by then, "lying in a balcony covered with several blankets," he wrote to a friend in 1939. "I heard repeated salvos in the town. I asked the reason. 'It is the hour of Lenin's funeral,'" he was told.

As he wrote in *My Life*, this high fever "paralyzed me at the most critical moments, and acted as my opponents' most steadfast ally." Doctors were never able to make a definitive diagnosis of his illness; at times, they believed it was a malaria attack. But Trotsky acknowledged that the timing of such fevers occurred "at the most critical moments," reinforcing the suspicion that the symptoms were the result of psychological vulnerability and not a microbe. Following Lenin's death, when the jockeying for power became overt, Trotsky failed to gather the strength to assert his presence on Red Square. As he admitted years later, "The fact of my absence at the mourning ceremonies [for Lenin] produced an uneasy impression on many of my friends." His physical weakness and lack of political resolve, combined with Stalin's treachery, undermined his stature in the country.

By the time of Lenin's death, Stalin, Kamenev, and Zinoviev were the preeminent leaders in the Kremlin. Trotsky was in eclipse. He was more than defeated. He was doomed.

5

Out of Power

THE SUCCESSION WAS not decided at the moment of Lenin's death. Kamenev and Zinoviev remained allied with Stalin, though both looked down on him. They were determined to prevent Trotsky from coming to power and were confident that their prestige among fellow Bolsheviks would guarantee their dominance. Kamenev, after all, led the party in Moscow, while Zinoviev headed the party in Leningrad and presided over the Comintern.*

Trotsky knew that he lacked a broad following within the party. Only days before Lenin's death a party conference had denounced his views as "a petty bourgeois deviation from Leninism." Hoping to restore his authority, he pledged his loy-

---

*The Communist International, or Comintern, was established in Moscow in 1919 for the purpose of uniting socialists who rejected the reform-minded policies of the Second International. It was always an instrument of Soviet foreign policy.

alty at the XIIIth Party Congress in May 1924. "I have never recognized freedom for groupings inside the party, nor do I recognize it now because under the present historical conditions groupings are merely another name for factions." Then Trotsky tried to ingratiate himself with a party that was changing before his eyes. "In the last analysis, the party is always right, because the party is the sole historical instrument the working class possesses for the solution of its fundamental tasks. . . . I know that no one can be right against the party. It is possible to be right only with the party and through it since history has not created any other way to determine the correct position." Trotsky, fearing humiliation and caught within a trap of his own making—a regime controlled by one dominant political party—was now compelled to compete for power within a system where his prestige was evaporating.

He looked for a way to assert his claim on Lenin's legacy. In the fall of 1924 he published his essay "The Lessons of October." Anxious to restore his rightful place in history, he described his role in the Bolshevik takeover as Lenin's principal collaborator. He also highlighted the failings of Kamenev and Zinoviev, who had disappointed Lenin in the spring of 1917, when they supported the Provisional Government, and then again in the fall, when they opposed an armed uprising. Lenin himself had urged the party to forgive their faults. But Trotsky—out of respect for historical truth or to settle scores—embarrassed them both. His strategy backfired. If Trotsky was ready to dredge up the failings of his rivals, they could hardly be expected to ignore his own.

Stalin took full advantage of the opportunity Trotsky had offered. He orchestrated attacks on "The Lessons of October," engaging in distortions of history that later ripened into a full-scale assault on historical truth: Stalin, not Trotsky, had been at the center of the Bolsheviks' military planning. Stalin, not Trotsky, had directed the armed units who took over the Winter Palace. With Stalin's encouragement, Zinoviev publicly declared, "All the talk about the special part played by Comrade Trotsky is a legend which is spread by officious 'party' gossips."

Trotsky had asserted in "The Lessons of October" that a Bolshevik's behavior in 1917 was the crucial means of evaluating the credentials of any party militant. No one had worked more closely with Lenin than he. To counteract Trotsky's claim, Stalin and his allies unearthed Trotsky's disagreements with Lenin, beginning in 1903 and stretching all the way to 1918, when they argued over the treaty of Brest Litovsk, and to 1920, when they disagreed over the role of trade unions. Stalin's logic was compelling: No one had argued with Lenin as Trotsky had done; no one had insulted Lenin as Trotsky had done; therefore, no one had betrayed Lenin as Trotsky had done.

In his memoirs, Trotsky described Stalin's strategy as an exercise in "sheer invention" which "magnified [his disagreements with Lenin] . . . to astronomic proportions." When Lenin and Trotsky had ordered the MRC to seize control of Petrograd, Trotsky had remarked to Lenin that it was "necessary to keep a detailed record of the events of the revolution in order to avoid later distortions." Lenin responded presciently. "It doesn't matter," he told Trotsky. "They will lie without end." Lenin was right, but he did not anticipate that the lies would be directed by one of their own.

In 1925, the year after Lenin's death, Kamenev published a collection of material focusing on Trotsky's arguments with Lenin. The letters and articles were themselves genuine, but the collection was designed to undermine respect for Trotsky, particularly among new party members who lacked historical memory. At that time, enrollment in the Communist Party numbered around 400,000; more than half had joined between 1920 and 1924.

In the most widely cited letter, which Trotsky had sent to the Georgian Menshevik Nikolai Chkheidze from Vienna in

January 1913—just when Lenin had commandeered the title *Pravda* for his own newspaper—he referred to Lenin as "a professional exploiter of every weakness in the Russian workers' movement" and claimed that the "edifice of Leninism is presently built on lies and fabrications, and that it carries within itself the poisonous roots of its own decomposition."

Years later Trotsky ironically characterized this letter as "extracted from the garbage heap of émigré squabbles for the education of the younger members of the party." But it still put him on the defensive. He tried, in vain, to blunt its effect. It "cannot help but produce the most terrible impression on every party member, especially on any who did not go through the prewar factional struggle in the emigration." He recognized, though, that "such citations sound no less wild to me than they do for every other party member."

This episode helped isolate Trotsky politically at a time when Stalin was on the ascendant. Trotsky could no longer sustain his position as commissar of war; he resigned in January 1925. But Zinoviev was not satisfied and demanded Trotsky's expulsion from the Communist Party, a move that Stalin deemed too extreme and premature; he refused to go along. Granting clemency, Stalin said at the time, "The policy of cutting off heads is liable to be 'infectious': you cut off one head today, another tomorrow, a third day after, and then what will remain of the party?" (Stalin knew how to be patient and bided his time before making sure that his prophetic warning later came true.) Neither Kamenev nor Zinoviev could take advantage of Trotsky's deepening political isolation. They sustained their alliance with Stalin, but were now joined by Nikolai Bukharin. He offered a theoretical foundation for NEP and a program of gradual economic development, under a mixed system of private ownership and government controls. This program suited the country's mood after years of poverty and dislocation. Endorsed by Stalin, it also reinforced his image as a moderate party leader.

Stalin then offered another ideological challenge to Trotsky. In late 1924 he began to promote the idea of "socialism in one country." This contrasted with Trotsky's long-held belief —a belief Lenin had shared—that the revolution could not survive without the support of new socialist states in Europe. Here again, Trotsky found himself on unstable ground. He could no longer persuasively argue in defense of imminent revolution in Western Europe when the revolutionary wave had passed and showed no sign of reviving. Stalin argued otherwise. After years of upheaval, the country needed stability. After years of war and revolution, the country needed peace. It was Trotsky who advocated permanent revolution, as if the Soviet Union could not stand on its own feet without the assistance of outside forces. By denying the possibility of building socialism in one country, Trotsky appeared to question the capacity of the Soviet proletariat. "Socialism in one country" became a patriotic rallying cry, while the call for "permanent revolution" was turned into a radical and irresponsible act of adventurism. In the eyes of the party, Trotsky appeared trapped by a hopelessly optimistic belief in revolution. The country wanted peace; Trotsky offered glory.

The arguments of both Trotsky and Stalin reflected the country's hopeless situation. The Soviet Union remained a poor, economically underdeveloped country in comparison with the countries of Western Europe. The proletariat had succeeded in gaining control of the government, but the development of a socialist system of agricultural and industrial production was still a long way off. Trotsky, and Lenin as well, had firmly believed that the revolution would spark similar upheavals elsewhere. But when that failed to happen, Stalin's contention—that socialism could be built within the Soviet Union's own borders—offered an alternative and for many an attractive way forward. Stalin's argument also carried the additional advantage once again of making him appear to be a moderate figure whose policies matched the mood of the country. There was no indication of the extreme measures he would soon implement to carry out his plans.

More important, Trotsky continued to underestimate Stalin. For Trotsky, Stalin was a marginal figure in the revolution. When he wrote his biography of Stalin in the 1930s, Trotsky engaged in a systematic review of party history—of congresses, conferences, the founding and dissolution of newspapers, of clandestine correspondence and meetings—all to demonstrate how modest a role Stalin had played in the years between 1904 and 1917. Trotsky was happy to dismiss him as "the outstanding mediocrity in our Party." Stalin was not an intellectual, but he was a master of political intrigue; Trotsky was the one who was out of his depth. His brilliant essays and books did not endear him to rank-and-file party members, particularly new ones who were joining a party being shaped by Stalin's values. As Trotsky wrote in *My Life*, "The apparatus was rapidly discovering that Stalin was flesh of its flesh." Still, Lenin's Testament continued to cast a shadow over Stalin's pre-eminence. But even here, armed with a loaded gun, Trotsky could not bring himself to take Stalin down.

His friend Max Eastman, back in New York, published a brief account in 1925 of what he had witnessed in Moscow earlier in the decade. Entitled *Since Lenin Died*, it was among the first to describe the struggle for power, the cynical assaults on Trotsky's reputation, and a candid evaluation of Trotsky's lack of ability "to gather people around him." At Trotsky's request, Eastman also included portions of Lenin's Testament in the volume, hoping to gain the attention of the worldwide Communist movement. But Trotsky, under pressure from the Politburo, disavowed Eastman's book and asserted that the Testament was a fabrication. Once again, he chose to submit and accept the humiliation of publicly lying rather than to press an obvious advantage.

Stalin also resorted to anti-Jewish prejudice to ensure Trotsky's defeat. In 1917 Trotsky had feared that enemies of the revolution would use his origin to discredit the Bolsheviks. But Trotsky never anticipated how Stalin would make use of "Bronstein." In March 1926 Trotsky learned that party bureaucrats were maligning him with antisemitic slanders. He appealed in writing to Bukharin, hoping that he would intervene. Trotsky described "a half-concealed struggle employing all kinds of tricks and allusions," creating the impression that "kikes within the Politburo are making a row." But members of the Communist Party were afraid to inform party organs about the Black Hundred agitation, "thinking that they, and not the Black Hundred, will be thrown out." "Is it true," Trotsky asked Bukharin, "is it possible that in our party, in Moscow, in workers' cells, antisemitic agitation should be carried out with impunity?" Trotsky's note conveys his naive surprise. The revolution had triumphed, the autocracy and its prejudices had been discarded, yet Trotsky could not rid himself of the handicap of being a Jew. Whatever Bukharin may have thought about Trotsky's appeal, he failed to respond.

In the meantime, Stalin continued to press Trotsky, making it difficult for him to rally his followers. His fevers, too, continued to plague him. In the spring of 1926 the Politburo discussed allowing Trotsky to seek medical treatment in Berlin. The party leadership and the secret police both advised against it, fearing either an attack on Trotsky or an attempt on his part to rally opponents of Stalin in Europe. The idea of forcing him out of the country "had not yet dawned within the policeman's skull of Stalin," Trotsky wrote in *My Life*. The Politburo left the decision to Trotsky; after consulting with friends, he and his wife departed for Berlin, traveling with false diplomatic passports under the name of a Ukrainian official. But the medical care in Germany proved to be useless. At the insistence of one surgeon, Trotsky underwent a tonsillectomy, which he recalled as the unpleasant experience of lying on a table and choking "on one's own blood." But the fever continued to recur. While Trotsky was recovering from the surgery, the police alerted him to an alleged assassination attempt by German monarchists. After the clinic was cordoned off, Trotsky was compelled to seek refuge in the Soviet embassy. German police never substantiated the claim, and he soon left Berlin wondering whether such a plot had ever really existed.

With Trotsky's star in eclipse, Stalin was also pushing aside Kamenev and Zinoviev. Their geographic bases were proving to be no match for Stalin's preeminence. By early 1926, neither Kamenev in Moscow nor Zinoviev in Leningrad was a party chief any longer; both men also lost their positions on the Politburo. Finally determined to confront Stalin, they formed a new alliance with Trotsky—the Joint Opposition—hoping to challenge Stalin within the party.

Events outside the country gave them unexpected openings. In May 1926 a general strike broke out in England in solidarity with striking British coal miners. Stalin and the Politburo lent support to the Trade Union Council, which meant that the Communist Party and its sympathizers would also support the union leadership. But then the Trade Union Council, unnerved by the effectiveness of the general strike, called it off after nine days without gaining substantial concessions from the mine owners or the government. Now the strike turned into an embarrassing failure for the left. Trotsky and the Joint Opposition accused Stalin of incompetent leadership: by supporting union leaders who were too prone to compromise, the Politburo had squandered a substantial opportunity for revolutionary change.

Another crisis unfolded in 1926 and 1927, as Stalin was pursuing a complex policy. With revolution closed off in Europe, the Kremlin saw an opportunity for revolutionary upheaval in Asia. The dominant party in China, the nationalist

Kuomintang led by Chiang Kai-shek, welcomed an alliance with a much smaller and weaker Communist movement. Stalin believed Chiang would not turn on his Communist allies. He instructed them to join forces with Chiang, confident that they could then undermine Chiang's leadership inside the Kuomintang. Trotsky thought otherwise, convinced that the Communists would be better off remaining independent from a bourgeois political movement, advice that resembled his criticism of Kremlin policy during the British general strike. His concerns in China proved to be justified. Faced with an attempt by workers and Communist allies to seize control of Shanghai in April 1927, Chiang's superior forces intervened and crushed them, leading to a large-scale massacre. (André Malraux immortalized these events in his novel *Man's Fate*.) Nonetheless, the Kremlin advised the Chinese Communist party to remain within the Kuomintang. Stalin's foreign policy turned out to be fatal for fellow revolutionaries. Trotsky, ever on the lookout to expose Stalin's incompetence and the disastrous results of his policies, pressed his advantage. He wrote appeals, circulated letters, and otherwise campaigned to raise the issue within the party and the Comintern. His followers, though, were reduced to arranging informal meetings in factories, private apartments, and student dormitories. Trotsky may even have considered creating a new and separate party to rival Stalin's. None of this maneuvering led anywhere.

The Joint Opposition continued to look for ways to undermine Stalin. One initiative was an attempt to get Lenin's Testament published in the Soviet Union. When this failed, it was the Joint Opposition, no doubt with Trotsky's agreement, that passed along the full text to the West. Max Eastman first published the Testament in the *New York Times* on October 18, 1926. Within days, Stalin went on the counteroffensive, denouncing the Joint Opposition as a "social-democratic deviation" and insisting that its leaders recant their views. Trotsky was not intimidated. In front of members of the Central Committee, he condemned Stalin as "the gravedigger of the revolution." Unnerved and furious, Stalin left the hall. The next morning, the Central Committee voted to remove Trotsky from the Politburo. His friends expressed their fears to him. Yury Pyatakov warned that "Stalin will never forgive him until the third and fourth generation." It was a prescient warning, but at the time neither Trotsky nor his wife took it seriously.

By the fall of 1927, Trotsky, Kamenev, and Zinoviev had been expelled from the party, along with hundreds of their followers. (According to Trotsky, Nadezhda Krupskaya told a group of opposition figures in 1926 that Stalin would have imprisoned Lenin had he still been alive.) That year the director Sergei Eisenstein lampooned Trotsky in the iconic film *October*, his account of the revolution, portraying him as an effete intellectual figure who had had little impact on the events around him. Humiliated, neither Kamenev nor Zinoviev could go on outside the fold. They recanted their views, imploring Stalin to restore their party membership, a request he granted. Trotsky was forced to vacate his Kremlin apartment, but Stalin had something more drastic in mind for him: deportation from Moscow to Central Asia.*

---

*In one indication of how confusing the political situation seemed to Western observers, the *New York Times*, anticipating Trotsky's exile, commented that "the ousted Opposition stood for the perpetuation of the ideas and conditions that have cut off Russia from Western civilization." Stalin was to be preferred, for he was moving "Russia in the direction of sanity." See *New York Times*, January 1, 1928, E4. Such an attitude was surprisingly widespread in the West. Abraham Cahan, the legendary editor of the *Forverts* in New York, wrote to a friend in September 1926 that he was satisfied with Stalin's victory over the "wild, bloodthirsty tactics and rhetoric of Zinoviev and Trotsky." For Cahan, Stalin's ascendancy would improve chances for democratic development in the Soviet Union and for the regime's relationship with the international socialist movement. He later regretted his misjudgment.

Trotsky and his family did not submit easily. One of his followers, the revolutionary writer Victor Serge, visited Trotsky in the days before his exile. "Watched day and night by comrades who were themselves watched by stool-pigeons,"

> Trotsky worked in a small room facing the courtyard and furnished only with a field bed and a table. . . . Dressed in a well-worn jacket, active and majestic, his high crop of hair almost white, his complexion sickly, he displayed in this cage a stubborn energy. In the next room messages which he had dictated were being typed out. In the dining room comrades arriving from every corner of the country were received—he talked with them hurriedly between telephone calls. All might be arrested any moment—what next? Nobody knew . . . but all were in a hurry to benefit from these last hours, for surely they were the last.

Trotsky and his family were scheduled to leave late on the evening of January 16, 1928. Thousands of his followers, alerted to the time, crowded the railroad tracks in front of the train that was supposed to take him away. The regime backed down and called to say that his deportation was being postponed for two days. But then armed officers came the next morning, catching Trotsky off guard. Trotsky barricaded himself in the apartment, refusing to give in and compelling the detachment to break down the door. One of the officers turned out to be a soldier who had served as a bodyguard for Trotsky during the war. Embarrassed and confused, he pleaded with Trotsky to shoot him; Trotsky could only comfort the fellow and encourage him to carry out orders. His passive resistance continued. He refused to dress himself, leaving his jailers no choice but to change his clothes. He refused to walk out on his own, compelling them to carry him out the door and down the stairs to the street. They took Trotsky and his family to the Kazan station, not the one where his followers had gathered the night before. Again, Trotsky refused to go on his own to the carriage; again he was carried by the armed escort. His sons were with him. His younger son, Sergei, struck one of the armed guards with his fist. His older son, Lev, tried to alert the railroad workers, as if they might intervene or raise a protest. But no one lifted a finger. Trotsky had first come to Moscow in 1899, a young revolutionary, shunted from a prison in Odessa to another in Moscow, from where tsarist policemen sent him and his wife to Siberia. Now he was being exiled again, but this time he would never return.

Trotsky had twice experienced the pleasures of Russian exile under Tsar Nicholas II: the interminable train ride deep into Siberia, the uncertainty of knowing one's destination, and police surveillance. But now it was the Soviet regime that was organizing his banishment. When they reached Samara on January 18, Trotsky sent an angry telegram to secret police headquarters in Moscow.

> When I was arrested in various countries, it was never covered with deception. The GPU is piling up confusion and deceit. I was told that I would be leaving on Wednesday evening, but they took me on Tuesday morning, leaving behind our personal things or necessary medicine. In a written notice, it was said I was being taken to Alma Ata, but on the way they changed it to Tashkent, from where, apparently, they will send us to a more distant point. In this way, I am going with an ill wife without linens, without medications, and without hope of receiving them soon.

The soldiers, though, were considerate and along the way brought him necessary clothes, towels, and soap. His sons initially joined them, but Sergei, determined to finish his engineering education, returned to the capital from the train's first stop not far from Moscow. Lev continued with his parents. Once the group reached Frunze, it took a week over mountains and through deep snow to make their way by bus, truck, sleigh, and on foot to Alma Ata, the capital of the Soviet republic of Kazakhstan.

It was here that Trotsky spent his final year in the Soviet Union. Although he remained under close surveillance, the regime had yet to impose a system of thorough control. He carried out an extensive correspondence with followers, many of whom were enduring exile in Siberia. From their letters, he understood that his banishment had been accompanied by hundreds, if not thousands of arrests. A group of Trotskyists in Siberia described humiliating conditions in prison and isolation cells: fifty-three prisoners were crammed into a ward designed to hold twenty-five. They were placed with "speculators, dealers in foreign currency, contrabandists, murderers, spies, counterfeiters, bribe takers, bandits, thieves, occultists, and embezzlers." Trotsky responded as best he could, eager to discuss the country's economic policies, its foreign relations, the ins and outs of discussions within the party itself.

He also sent frequent protests to police and party officials in Moscow, appealing for changes in his accommodations or the terms of his exile. He was not in prison or subjected to physical torture, but he had a taste of the humiliation that Stalin liked to mete out. Initially, he and his family stayed in a hotel, but they had no kitchen and lacked necessary funds for eating in a restaurant. "It is possible to create conditions of imprisonment in Moscow and no point to exile me four thousand versts [2,600 miles]," Trotsky protested in a telegram. He was in Alma Ata for hardly a week when he wrote to officials in Moscow insisting that he be permitted to go hunting beyond the narrow radius that had been designated by local officials; his request was granted. He looked forward to hunting "quail, little bustards, snow leopards, tigers." But the tigers were too far away, and he promised not to threaten them.

His exile to Alma Ata and then subsequently to Turkey set the stage for the profound political and psychological pressures that shaped his work. Trotsky began to write his memoirs in Alma Ata. Stalin had permitted him to transfer his archives to Central Asia; they actually followed him by truck in several large, unwieldy wooden crates. But these documents were not sufficient for his purposes, and he found himself plying his daughter Zinaida, his son Sergei, and other family members for books, journals, pamphlets, and newspapers, including hard-to-find volumes. Out of power and secluded, Trotsky put his formidable energy into his literary projects. He needed assistance, though, and he was not someone to spare others, including his children.

At the same time, he and his wife tried to sustain their family life. Lev remained with them, helping his father after Trotsky's two personal secretaries were forbidden to remain in Central Asia. There were many letters and telegrams from Leningrad and Moscow, with updates about family matters, health concerns, and doses of quinine for Natalia Sedova, who was exhibiting symptoms of malaria. Trotsky also heard from his sister Olga, who was now divorced from Lev Kamenev. Olga was having difficulties at work, and her letters hint that her connection to her ostracized brother was the root of her troubles. On February 20 Zinaida sent unsettling news about her younger sister, Nina. "Ninushka has gotten very sick, a terrible cold. The doctor thinks she has tuberculosis and wants her to consider a sanatorium, where she can go outside. She needs an X-ray to clarify the conditions of her lungs." Zinaida's own life was growing precarious. She had lost her job as a teacher "out of fear she will instill Trotskyism and educate in the spirit of 'neo-Menshevism.'"

That May, Trotsky exchanged letters with his first wife, Alexandra Sokolovskaya. She wrote to him from Leningrad, where, living near their daughters, she closely followed news about him. "Dear Friend," she wrote. "You know that all my political sympathies always coincide with yours." She had been questioned at the time of her own recent expulsion from the party and described the interrogation for him. "You are even against the expulsion of Trotsky," they told her. "I have known Trotsky for thirty years as the most ardent revolutionary," she had responded. "He has always stood by his positions and not even for an instant has he changed them." Sokolovskaya knew that he had written to Zinaida requesting a long list of books. Now Sokolovskaya had taken on the work; she had already sent him the memoirs of Count Witte but was having difficulty finding other books about the 1880s and 1890s. She also asked him to write about his life in Alma Ata and voiced concern that he was living in a malaria-infested region.

Nina had been sick for the past two months with "something like malaria," her letter continued; she had been hospitalized twice, but as yet there was no definitive diagnosis. Thinking about their daughters, Sokolovskaya voiced despair over their future. "How will they live in this world?" she asked Trotsky. She had recently received copies of two letters which he had sent to her while she was in prison in Odessa thirty years before. "Right away they restored to memory things that happened long, long ago." Her gentle feelings were evident. Trotsky responded later in May. His tone was businesslike; he did not refer to their shared memories. He needed the books because he was beginning to write his memoirs. She could send them in Russian, French, German, or English, while reports or brochures could be sent in additional languages, like Italian or Spanish, even in the Balkan languages. He was grateful for her assistance but did not reciprocate her tenderness. Two weeks later, Trotsky learned that Nina had died of tuberculosis in Leningrad; he was not permitted to attend her funeral. She left a son and a daughter, while her husband, Man Nevelson, remained in Siberian exile.

As the year progressed, Stalin began to shift his strategies. At the time of Trotsky's exile, Stalin was still allied with Bukharin, but by the summer of 1928 the regime had begun to adopt the extreme measures that led to the first Five Year Plan: rapid industrialization and, most ominously, the forced collectivization of agriculture. Dubbed the "Left Course," these policies resembled a more brutal version of Trotsky's own. By abandoning NEP, Stalin was initiating an impatient push for economic modernization at the expense of the peasants.

The evolving political reality compounded Trotsky's personal tragedy. Not all his followers remained steadfast. Isolated in Alma Ata, Trotsky learned about the compromises of onetime allies and friends. Yury Pyatakov, Anton Antonov-Ovseenko, Karl Radek, and Yevgeny Preobrazhensky, among others, made their peace with Stalin's policies and abandoned the Opposition. News about other arrests reached him from Moscow and Kharkov, and from cities in Siberia. In June a group of Moscow Trotskyists described for him the arrest of "worker-Bolsheviks" in the capital. They decried the state of democracy in the party. "It is impossible to implant democracy from above and by decree," they wrote to him. "We need to throw out not only drunkards and bribe takers, but all the bureaucrats and opportunists. . . . And we need to immediately stop any acts of repression, exile, and arrests."

By the fall, the regime began to tighten its controls on Trotsky himself. Between April and October, he had dispatched eight hundred political letters and five hundred telegrams, while he had received one thousand letters and seven hundred telegrams, most of them signed collectively. Each letter was copied and analyzed, then summarized for Stalin. The regime could no longer tolerate such a resolute connection between Trotsky and his followers. Letters and telegrams to and from friends and supporters were no longer delivered. And a courier who had been discreetly taking and delivering written messages was identified and arrested. Trotsky longed to hear from Zinaida, but her letters, too, failed to reach him. "Since the end of October," Sedova wrote to a friend, "we are under a postal block-ade. Things will not stop at this, of course. We are awaiting something worse." Stalin was not done with them.

He could no longer bear Trotsky's presence in the Soviet Union, but the Politburo balked at expelling Trotsky from the country. At a meeting in mid-January, three members voted against expulsion, and according to some reports Bukharin broke down in tears, overcome by guilt over his own earlier be-havior toward Trotsky. Perhaps, as well, Bukharin experienced a feeling of foreboding over what Stalin would do next—to Trotsky, to himself, to any of them. Their opposition notwith-standing, Stalin pushed through the decision. Trotsky learned about the expulsion order on January 20, 1929. He was charged with "counterrevolutionary activity expressing itself in the or-ganization of an illegal anti-Soviet party, whose activity has lately been directed toward provoking anti-Soviet actions and preparing for an armed struggle against Soviet power."

Two days later, Trotsky, his wife, and their son Lev were taken by an armed escort and placed in a bus which took them to the Kurday mountain range. Faced with heavy snowstorms, the group was assigned a special tractor to tow seven vehicles through the Kurday pass. "During the snowstorms," Trotsky reported, "seven men and a good many horses were frozen to death on the pass. We were obliged to transfer to sleighs." It took them seven hours to travel nineteen miles. A railway car brought them near Moscow, where, at his insistence, his younger son and Lev's wife were able to join them. Trotsky was informed that he was being expelled to Constantinople. He re-fused to acquiesce to the decree, insisting that he be sent to Germany. For some reason the regime hesitated, leaving him and his family alone in a railway carriage for twelve days and nights while it sorted out what to do next. Food and fuel were delivered at regular intervals, but the exiles were not permitted to leave the train. They read French novels and a history of

Russia, played chess, and received newspapers that told them about the arrests of hundreds of Trotskyists. It was only on February 8 that an official informed Trotsky of Germany's refusal to accept him. With or without his agreement, he was being taken to Turkey.

It took two days for a larger train to carry them southward to Odessa, where Sergei bade them farewell and returned to Moscow. They would never see him again. The train brought them directly to the harbor, where they boarded a steamer, the *Ilyich*—Lenin's patronymic—which required the assistance of an icebreaker to move through the Black Sea for the first sixty miles. Trotsky and his wife, along with Lev, were the only passengers on board, accompanied by two secret police agents to ensure their isolation.

The Kremlin remained silent about the expulsion, while rumors abounded in the Western press. European Communist newspapers reported that Trotsky was leaving the country voluntarily, perhaps on an official or semiofficial mission, with a sizable entourage. This was deliberate misinformation. Late in January 1929 the *New York Times* began reporting on the arrest of Trotsky's followers: there was a "war against Trotsky" leading to the arrest of "waverers who stood at the crossroads"; they would be sent to "rigorous isolation." Walter Duranty, the *Times'* principal correspondent, whose coverage of the Soviet Union has since come under withering criticism for its unquestioned acceptance of Stalin's propaganda, commented in a front-page article that those under arrest had been planning a civil war and had set up an underground press. Trotsky, moreover, was "said to be head of an army on the Afghan border," a claim with no basis in reality. For Duranty, Trotsky was the "most dangerous firebrand in the eyes of the world." In early February, Duranty cited official claims that Trotsky had been circulating subversive handbills and had established an "underground railroad" to distribute his letters. So Stalin had decided

to exile him much in the way Lenin had sent his former colleagues—like the Menshevik leaders Yuli Martov and Fyodor
Dan—out of the country. Within days, the *Times* reported,
once more on the front page, that Trotsky was missing on
board a ship during a "terrific blizzard and hurricane" in the
Black Sea; his whereabouts remained a "mystery," and there
were fears (or was it hopes?) that he would not reach his destination alive.*

The truth was far more ordinary. The regime had made no
announcement of its plans in order to prevent the kind of demonstrations that had occurred in Moscow when Trotsky was
sent off to Alma Ata. Stalin also wanted to keep his options
open; he even considered Trotsky's request to be sent to Germany, and only after Germany refused entry to Trotsky was he
spirited away to Turkey. As they arrived in Turkey, Trotsky was
handed an envelope containing $1,500, an insulting amount of
money to give to the leader of the revolution and the founder
of the Red Army. But Trotsky was virtually penniless; he swallowed his pride and accepted the envelope. Upon arrival in
Turkey, he protested the conditions of his exile, believing that
Stalin and the government of Mustafa Kemal Atatürk were cooperating in a conspiracy against him. But Turkish officials
guaranteed his safety and welcomed him as their guest. Hoping to save a revolution he had helped to make, Trotsky intended to rally like-minded radicals and Communists in the
West. Stalin, he was confident, could still be toppled.

---

*In a letter to one of his American followers, Herbert Solow, on October
27, 1937, Trotsky referred to Duranty as "one of the most miserable liars of
the modern press."

6

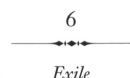

Exile

POLITICALLY, TROTSKY WAS a spent force, yet he continued to command attention. The image of an exiled revolutionary, Lenin's closest collaborator, haunted the capitals and chancelleries of Europe.

Trotsky fell back on a strategy that had once succeeded. He pulled together a new network of militant Marxists like himself to challenge the commissars in the Kremlin, in the same way that he and Lenin had confronted first the tsar and then the Provisional Government. Trotsky, though, was not facing a crumbling, disoriented monarchy but a ruthless machine that understood conspiracy firsthand—that had, in fact, gone through the same history as Trotsky. This time, a small group of disaffected, isolated revolutionaries did not stand a chance.

Trotsky spent several weeks in the Soviet consulate in Constantinople, where to his surprise he was treated with deference and respect. The Western press was eager to hear from him.

He obliged with articles in British and American newspapers, including four dispatches in the *New York Times*. Trotsky did not restrain himself: he described Stalin's successful maneuvers to gain power while Lenin lay dying; the conditions of his exile in Alma Ata; and the arrests of other onetime Bolshevik leaders. He also repeated his description of Stalin as "the grave-digger of the revolution." Only after these articles appeared did the Kremlin react publicly to Trotsky's expulsion. To explain its actions, Moscow newspapers claimed that Trotsky had "employed illegal printing presses," wanted "people to join anti-Soviet demonstrations," and "was and remains a Menshevik." It is hard to believe that such flimsy accusations could have convinced a neutral observer of Trotsky's treachery. But Stalin was not concerned about Western public opinion; it was the Communist movement that needed an explanation. Branded a Menshevik, Trotsky could be relegated to the same "dustbin of history" where he had consigned Yuli Martov.

His expulsion sent shivers through radical circles nonetheless. In New York that April, the *Times* reported that forty "Stalinites" invaded a social club on the upper East Side where Trotskyists were meeting. They came "armed with brass knuckles, knives and long strips of rubber hose." According to this account, "When police reserves ended the battle, one man was found to have been probably fatally stabbed, eight teeth were discovered strewn on the speakers' platform and six men's coats and women's dresses were in ruins on the floor." Similar outbreaks of violence between followers of Stalin and of Trotsky occurred throughout Europe.

Compelled to vacate his rooms in the consulate, Trotsky moved to a hotel. For several weeks, he tried to secure a visa to a Western European country. Everywhere he turned, democratic governments rejected him. The Netherlands did not accept him, although it had welcomed German kaiser Wilhelm II in 1918, then refused to relinquish him to the Allies when they sought to try him for war crimes. France pointed to Trotsky's expulsion in 1916, reminding him that the order had never been rescinded. Norway declared its respect for the right of asylum, but expressed anxiety about his safety. Another report claimed that Trotsky had asked Maxim Gorky to intervene on his behalf with Italian officials, hoping he could join Gorky on Capri; nothing came of it.

His attempts to enter Germany also led nowhere. Communists expressed their hatred for him, pledging "to make Trotsky harmless as soon as he crosses the German frontier." Nazi leaders, as well, in one of their journals, the *Illustrierte Beobachter* (Illustrated observer), wrote, "Trotsky, the Soviet Jewish bloodhound, wishes to reside in Berlin during his exile. We shall have to keep a vigilant eye on this Jewish assassin and criminal." Two months later, the Nazis warned that if Trotsky were to come to Germany, he "would be shot down like a mad dog." In the end Germany, too, turned Trotsky away; as the *New York Times* reported, it "might find itself unable to expel him, once admitted, should his presence become objectionable."

He placed his hopes on England. George Bernard Shaw, H. G. Wells, and John Maynard Keynes issued appeals on his behalf. Other prominent figures, like Rudyard Kipling and the scientist Sir Ernest Rutherford, refused outright to add their voices. The British government preferred to avoid controversy and turned him away. For Shaw, "those who had an unreasoning dread of [Trotsky] as a caged lion" should allow him to enter Britain "if only to hold the key to his cage." Fed up, Shaw declared that a Turkish government was setting an "example of liberality" to a British one.

For Trotsky, all this frustration proved to be a useful lesson in the ways of Western democracies. "The democratic and Social Democratic press [in Germany]," he wrote in *My Life*, "derived malicious satisfaction from pointing out the fact that a believer in the revolutionary dictatorship was obliged to seek asylum in a democratic country." He continued to press for a visa, sending appeals to governments and public figures, hoping to find refuge closer to the center of political life, all to no avail. "On many sides it has been explained to me that my disbelief in democracy is my greatest sin," Trotsky observed, "but when I ask to be given a brief object lesson in democracy, there are no volunteers."

By April, Lev Sedov found a secure home for his parents on the island of Prinkipo in the Sea of Marmara, an hour-and-a-half boat ride from Constantinople. Trotsky adjusted to his new life in a "spacious, dilapidated villa rented from a bankrupt pasha," as Isaac Deutscher described it. Turkish authorities proved to be gracious hosts. They provided guards at the villa to protect him from Stalinist agents and White émigrés bent on revenge; they never interfered with a steady stream of visitors and correspondence. Within weeks, he celebrated May Day with a visit by the British socialists Sidney and Beatrice Webb. In Moscow, though, the Kremlin sustained its crude attacks on him. The May Day parade through Red Square featured two floats with caricatures of Trotsky: on one he was depicted "as a centaur bearing on his back Sir Austen Chamberlain, the British Foreign Secretary, complete with monocle and high hat"; on the other he was dressed in a peasant costume dancing to music played by bourgeois capitalists.

False reports in the Western press served to confound public opinion. In July 1929, for example, the *New York Times* carried an article claiming that Trotsky's exile to Turkey was all a ruse: "The whole story of bad blood between Stalin and Trotsky has been a blind for the purpose of paving the way for Trotsky to play the Communist game in European capitals." The dispatch concluded that Trotsky was "in constant communication with Stalin" and would soon return to Moscow now that the scheme he and Stalin had cooked up—to roil European countries—had failed.

Trotsky feared that the government of Kemal Atatürk would grow weary of hosting him. But Turkey remained a reliable haven. Trotsky remained there for four and a half years, a time that proved to be unusually productive. (After the Kremlin deprived him and his family of Soviet citizenship in February 1932, Turkey offered travel documents, making his subsequent trips possible.) To earn a living, he arranged contracts for his memoirs and an account of the revolution. Western publishers paid him tens of thousands of dollars, enough for Trotsky to hire secretaries and translators, to employ a cook and a housecleaner, and to offer support to small groups of followers in the West. Over the next decade, Trotsky corresponded with dozens of them. He devoted considerable time to advising, encouraging, rebuking, orienting them left, orienting them right—all with the goal of trying to forge a viable movement. This was draining work and only a determined revolutionary could sustain such an effort. To relax, he enjoyed the outdoors, taking long and strenuous boat rides to hunt on other islands or go deep sea fishing.

By July, Trotsky had started a new journal, the *Bulletin of the Opposition*, with the help of his son Lev. (That summer, Lev made a futile attempt to secure permission to return to Moscow to see his wife and son, whom he had left behind, but his request was denied.) The *Bulletin* was designed to rally followers and expose the criminal nature of Stalin's regime. Although its print run never exceeded a thousand, it was read within party circles, carried into the Soviet Union by diplomats and journalists. Stalin is said to have read each issue carefully. Stalin, in fact, was obsessed with Trotsky. According to the late Dmitri Volkogonov, who had access to tightly controlled material from Stalin's archive, he ordered nearly everything by or about Trotsky in the Western press to be translated for him. And he read Trotsky's work in Russian with great attention, often highlighting passages and leaving comments on the margins.

Trotsky used the *Bulletin* as an outlet for information coming from the Soviet Union and for his own analysis of political crises. Its scores of issues related the story of a decade. In the initial issue, Trotsky published a report from followers who were enduring hard labor in a Siberian camp near Tobolsk. Later in 1929, Trotsky's close friend and collaborator Christian Rakovsky observed (from his place of exile) how Stalin's shift in policy, his Left Course, was demoralizing Trotskyists.

Circulating the *Bulletin*, corresponding with followers all over Europe and North America, Trotsky was reverting to a familiar kind of political action. No doubt he believed that careful strategic maneuvering could weaken Stalin. Writing *My Life* at that time, he recalled his first revolutionary pamphlets when he produced material for workers in Nikolaev. "What a sorry, fantastic thing it would have seemed to imagine that [we] could, in this way, overthrow a mighty state that was centuries old!" Why couldn't a similar strategy work again? Since 1897, he recalled, "I have waged the fight chiefly with a pen in my hand." But Trotsky's writing never posed a threat to Stalin, even when Lev moved to Berlin in February 1931 to establish an editorial office for the *Bulletin*.

Just weeks before Lev's departure, Trotsky's older daughter, Zinaida, was able to reach Prinkipo along with her five-year-old son, Seva. Trotsky had invited her, and she hoped to find a place for herself within the Opposition, to work alongside her father as her half-brother Lev was doing. She had to leave behind her husband, Platon Volkov (who was in exile), and a daughter from a previous marriage. The girl was being cared for by her grandmother, Alexandra Sokolovskaya, who was also raising the two children of the deceased Nina. The extended family was only beginning its march to Golgotha.

During his years in Turkey, Trotsky watched two cataclysmic events unfold, one inside the Soviet Union and the other in Germany. With the advent of Stalin's first Five Year Plan, Trotsky learned about the devastating effects of forced collectivization. This was an enormous and cruel exercise in social engineering: the forced transfer of millions of peasants, who based their livelihoods on the cultivation of small plots of land, onto collective farms. It caused chaos in the countryside and resulted in the deaths of millions of peasants, among them *kulaks*, who were accused, often unfairly, of owning too much property and exploiting other peasants. It was a party axiom that at some point it would be necessary to squeeze the peasants in order to feed the cities, gain necessary taxes to support industrial growth, and make it possible for now superfluous farmhands to move to urban centers, where they could work in new factories and power plants. Much of this economic strategy resembled Trotsky's own. But he had advocated gradualist domestic policies; in 1920 he had pushed for NEP-like reforms to the economy, a full year before Lenin initiated a similar program. As collectivization began in late 1929, Trotsky voiced misgivings about its human toll, insisting that it should take place through slow and voluntary measures. He called for an end to dekulakization and even endorsed market mechanisms —which had been part of NEP—as a way to move the economy forward. Such statements, though, were also meant to differentiate himself from Stalin; Trotsky never did explain how simple persuasion could make reluctant, tradition-bound peasants move from their small holdings to large collective farms. In reality, with the advent of the Five Year Plan, many onetime followers abandoned their support for Trotsky and adopted Stalinism as their banner, recognizing that the Plan's proclaimed goals—particularly the emphasis on rapid industrialization—matched Trotsky's earlier rhetoric. This apparent similarity between Trotsky's economic strategy from earlier in the 1920s and Stalin's Left Course made it impossible for Trotsky and his followers to join with Bukharin, who opposed the

harsh, coercive elements of the first Five Year Plan; such an alliance might have challenged Stalin's monopoly on power.
Trotsky could also be inconsistent when it came to condemning the suffering associated with collectivization. Writing in
1936, he dismissed reports of mass violence. "At the present
time," he asserted, "hardly anybody would be foolish enough
to repeat the twaddle of liberals to the effect that collectivization as a whole was accomplished by naked force."

Trotsky faced fewer ideological dilemmas as he watched
Hitler's rise to power in Germany. Here he could readily see
the failure of Stalin's policies. By the late 1920s the Kremlin
had begun to instruct Western Communist Parties to refuse to
cooperate with Social Democrats, who were nothing more
than "social fascists," the ideological equivalent of the Nazis
themselves. In Germany this policy resulted in a great catastrophe. As Hitler's National Socialists grew in electoral strength,
Stalin's policies emasculated the left by deliberately dividing
Communist from Social Democrat; the results were tragic and
entirely foreseeable. Trotsky had nothing but contempt for
Stalin's policies and the attitude of former supporters, like Karl
Radek, who were now trumpeting Stalin's line. As Trotsky
wrote in the *Bulletin of the Opposition* with his usual acerbic wit:

> The differences between blondes and brunettes are not as
> great, in fact they are significantly less, than the differences
> between a human being and an ape. Anatomically and phys-
> iologically, blondes and brunettes belong to the same spe-
> cies; they can belong to the same nationality, even to the
> very same family. And finally, they both can be similar
> scoundrels. And still, skin color and hair color have signifi-
> cance, not only in a police passport, but in general in every-
> day life. Radek . . . wants to prove that a brunette is actually
> a blonde, but with dark skin and with black hair.

Trotsky remained consistent in his warnings about Germany. Should Hitler gain power, he saw the likelihood of a

general European war. Hitler was well aware of Trotsky's pre-
monition. In 1931, visited by editors from a conservative newspaper, Hitler ranted to them about his enemies, "banging his
fist on the table, sometimes shouting—about the communists,
the Vatican, the Jews, Freemasonry, the press, Karl Marx, Trotsky, and the city of Berlin."

Cut off from the Soviet Union, living in semi-isolation,
Trotsky devoted himself to writing. He had always been productive, but now he wrote to earn a living and to defend his
place in history. Stalin had begun his systematic distortion of
history, a calculated campaign to obscure and defame Trotsky's
role in the Bolshevik Revolution and to inflate his own. Trotsky responded to this campaign with his book *The Stalin School
of Falsification*. Relying on archival material, he published
speeches from Moscow in the 1920s and correspondence from
Lenin. He also revisited the events of the revolution to confirm
his primary role in the seizure of power.

His most enduring projects were his memoirs, *My Life*, and
the three-volume *History of the Russian Revolution*. Both were
widely read and translated; both were also exercises in politics.
Trotsky's account of the revolution played a major role in how
the events of 1917 would be remembered: swirling crowds,
heroic soldiers and sailors, a population carried along by History, pushed by its sufferings and pulled by its hopes.* He also
began a third major project, a biography of Stalin, later in the
1930s; it was left unfinished on his desk at the time of his assassination in August 1940.

These three books—his memoirs, his history of the revolution, and his account of Stalin's life—share one consistent
theme. Trotsky remained convinced—and committed to con-
vincing others—that the regime he and Lenin had sought to

---

*The Bolshevik myth notwithstanding, on the day following the coup,
most residents of Petrograd did not realize that the Provisional Government
had fallen and the Bolsheviks were taking control.

establish had never been intended to result in the kind of dictatorship Stalin was fashioning. This belief had both intensely personal and historical dimensions and was central to the dilemma Trotsky faced in exile. While he was documenting his role alongside Lenin in the creation of the first socialist state, he felt compelled to assert that they had some other kind of dictatorship in mind. In his eyes, Stalinism should not be considered a natural or inevitable consequence of Bolshevism. Trotsky could not accept the idea that Stalin might be Lenin's true heir and therefore, in a paradoxical way, his own. So he wrote vivid descriptions of Stalin's crimes and remained oblivious to Lenin's. He seemed to be haunted by the fear that he had helped to create the system that was destroying his family along with his dream of a socialist utopia. He argued that the violence he had unleashed to defend the revolution was supposed to subside once the Civil War was over and therefore could not be connected to the corrupt and self-serving purposes that guided Stalinism. Friedrich Engels had foreseen this dilemma. Writing in 1885 to Vera Zasulich, he observed, "People who boast that they *made* a revolution always see the day after that they had no idea what they were doing, that the revolution *made* does not in the least resemble the one they would like to make. That is what Hegel calls the irony of history, an irony which few historical personalities escape." This dilemma troubled Trotsky for the last decade of his life.

Trotsky enjoyed one unexpected trip during his time in Turkey. In late 1932 a group of left-wing Danish students invited him to present a lecture on the fifteenth anniversary of the Bolshevik Revolution. Learning of the invitation, the Danish monarchy expressed its opposition: the Bolsheviks had murdered two sons and the grandchildren of the Danish princess Dagmar, who became Russian empress and the mother of Nicholas II. Nonetheless, Trotsky and his wife sailed from

Constantinople on November 14, bound for Copenhagen. The European press followed his trip, all the while indulging in the wild speculation that he would discreetly meet an envoy from the Kremlin or embark on a conspiracy to overthrow Stalin. In reality, his trip reflected his isolation. Greek officials did not allow him to visit Athens. The Italian government (led by Mussolini) allowed him to disembark at Naples and under police escort visit the ruins at Pompeii. From there he traveled to Marseilles. French officials reacted nervously to his arrival. They compelled him to disembark at a point far from ordinary passengers. He was rushed by car and train to Dunkirk on the English Channel, where he boarded another ship for Denmark.

Trotsky delivered his lecture—a summary of his history of the revolution—to an audience of two thousand people. It was the last time he was ever to speak before a large crowd. Trotsky was the living embodiment of the Bolshevik Revolution, and his lecture, delivered in German, enthralled the audience. But the remainder of his eight-day stay in Denmark was uneventful. Under close police supervision, he hardly saw Copenhagen and in spite of strenuous efforts was not able to extend his stay or get permission to travel in the country. Dozens of followers from all over Europe came to see him. He also spent a good deal of time on the telephone with Lev in Berlin. Zinaida was now in Berlin as well. Trotsky had urged her to move there for treatment of a severe psychological disorder (she may have suffered from schizophrenia). Seva remained in Prinkipo, and Lev was increasingly clear with his parents that they could not send the boy to her; she was in no condition to care for him.

Unable to remain in Denmark, Trotsky headed by boat to Antwerp and then by train to Paris. French officials had assured him that he could remain briefly in Paris to see Lev, but once in the French capital, he was again abruptly compelled to leave. Trotsky spent just a few hours with Lev in Marseilles before he and Sedova were rushed onto a boat and taken to Italy. To their surprise and relief, the Italian Foreign Ministry granted them a transit visa. Once Trotsky reached Italy, the emotional upheaval connected to their trip took its toll. As Natalia Sedova wrote to Lev in Paris, "Papa and I sat for a long time in the dark compartment and wept." They were able to see Venice before finally returning to Prinkipo on December 12. Within weeks, their lives were shattered by personal and political tragedies.

In spite of Lev's warnings, in a misguided attempt to provide some grounding in Zinaida's life, Seva was sent to his mother in Berlin at the end of December. She was incapable of taking care of the boy. Moreover, the police were urging her to leave the country within a month, before German elections brought Hitler to power. She was also in despair over Trotsky's inability to welcome her warmly or to find a role for her in his work. She had long adored her father from afar. Now everything was collapsing around her. On January 5, burdened by depression, cut off from her husband, Zinaida barricaded the door to her apartment, then turned on the gas in her kitchen. Lev cabled his parents about his sister's fate. As Trotsky described it, the telegram expressed "unbearable moral tension with every line," as Lev sat "alone with the corpse of his elder sister." Lev was also able to telephone his brother in Moscow to break the news to him; it was the last time the doomed brothers spoke with each other. Trotsky blamed Stalin for Zinaida's death, emphasizing the loss of her homeland and her Soviet citizenship. He wrote to Zinaida's mother, Alexandra Sokolovskaya, to inform her of this latest calamity. "I strongly, strongly embrace your gray head and mix my tears with yours," he wrote to her. He and his wife went into seclusion, unable to leave their room, barely able to eat or communicate with the household. When Trotsky emerged a few days later, he looked much older, his hair much grayer.

Sokolovskaya's reply reached him at the end of August. She, too, was in despair over the death of her "radiant little dove." Looking at her grandchildren, she confided to Trotsky that she no longer believed in life and doubted that "they would grow up." She held Trotsky responsible for Zinaida's death. Zinaida had needed more from him: more time, attention, and love. Sokolovskaya had recognized how fragile both Nina and Zinaida were in early 1928, when their father was sent to Alma Ata and their physical and emotional well-being were in question. "How will they live in this world?" she had asked him. He had no answer. Five years later, both daughters were dead.

Events in Germany compounded his despair. By the end of January, Hitler had become chancellor of Germany. Trotsky grew anxious for Lev. The Nazis banned the *Bulletin*, and Lev, fearing for his life, went into hiding. He had to get out of Germany; sometime in March he was able to reach Paris.

First from Turkey and then from France, where he moved in July 1933, Trotsky steadily composed denunciations of Hitler and of Stalin. With Hitler in power, "the world of Versailles has finally turned into a madhouse," Trotsky wrote. It was Stalin's responsibility, for "the politics of the Communist Party was a complete sham. Its leadership proceeded from the absurd notion that Social Democracy and National Socialism present two varieties of fascism, as if, following Stalin's ill-starred formula, they 'are not opposites, but twins.'" The Comintern liked to declare that its policies had been above reproach and dismiss the significance of Hitler's victory. But Trotsky knew better. In his eyes, Hitler's victory was a decisive setback to Europe's working class. "Yes, five million Communists still managed, each individually, to make their way to the polling booths," Trotsky wrote in the *Bulletin of the Opposition*. "But in the factories and the streets their presence is not felt. . . . The bureaucratic terror of Stalinism has paralyzed their will even before the gangster terror of fascism has started its work."

Trotsky had no illusions about Hitler, and he questioned

whether Stalin would prove a reliable opponent of Nazism. But he was still loyal to the Soviet Union. In March 1933 Trotsky offered his personal assistance to members of the Politburo. Stalin, he wrote to them, was leading the country to disaster, and he compared him to Kerensky and to the Spanish dictator Primo de Rivera on the eve of their governments' collapse. "I consider it my duty to make one more attempt to appeal to a feeling of responsibility of those who rule the Soviet government today." But no one responded.

Although Trotsky's years in Turkey were the most productive of his time in exile, he longed to move closer to the center of European political life. He had lived in France before and he was determined to seek asylum there. Assisted by numerous friends, Trotsky succeeded in having his expulsion order from 1916 rescinded. Permission to reside in France was granted, but the arrangements carried significant restrictions: he could not visit Paris, and he had to live in a southern district, refrain from public presentations and from revealing his identity, and accept close police supervision. It is hard to say whether such conditions were meant to protect Trotsky or reflected a genuine fear that he could overthrow the French republic.

With his wife and three secretaries, Trotsky reached Marseilles in mid-July; from there, they moved to St. Palais, a small town on the Atlantic coast, where they stayed for several months. Lev insisted on such substantial precautions that neither the press nor Stalinist agents knew where Trotsky was. With Lev's assistance, several prominent writers and intellectuals came to visit. André Malraux spent an afternoon with Trotsky; Simone Weil also came by. They kept their visits discreet and did not divulge where they saw him. The French government, impressed by Trotsky's low profile, relaxed its restrictions and permitted him to move to Barbizon, closer to Paris. But concerns for his safety remained. To see him, visitors had to pass through an elaborate ring of security. One British leftist wrote a description of being taken to see Trotsky in 1934. "It was all rather breathtaking," he recalled.

> Driven at midnight to a station in Paris, put on a train but kept ignorant of our destination, leaving the train according to instructions at a certain time, recognized by a comrade armed with a telegraphed description of us, whirled off for a further journey, admitted past various obstacles, and finally greeted with tempestuous heartiness by Leon Trotsky himself. The atmosphere of conspiratorial secrecy, which would have thrilled our school days, was merely a grim reminder that repeated threats of assassination necessitated these inconvenient precautions.

In spite of such safeguards, Trotsky's identity would sometimes slip out, and then the press would descend on him. Hounded out of a refuge, he had to move from one city to another; eventually he and his wife lived quietly for almost a year in a remote village in the Alps, near Grenoble, without secretaries or bodyguards in the home of a schoolteacher. He could read but was hardly able to write at all.

Trotsky was in France when he learned that his younger son, Sergei Sedov, had been arrested in Moscow in March 1935. Sergei was caught up in the wave of repression that emerged after the assassination of the Leningrad party leader Sergei Kirov on December 1, 1934. Within months, the party began a comprehensive purge of all former followers of Zinoviev, Kamenev, and Trotsky. Trotsky followed the aftermath of Kirov's murder with alarm, sensing that Stalin would exploit the incident for his own ruthless purposes. Sergei Sedov was an engineer. He had remained in the Soviet Union to pursue his studies, convinced that his indifference to politics provided a margin of safety. Following Sergei's arrest, the Kremlin voiced public assurances that he was not in a prison but under "supervision" in order to prevent contact with his parents. According to Sedova, they had exchanged only banal messages about each other's health. She tried to send some money to his wife, a librarian in Moscow, but the Norwegian bank returned the money because the "beneficiary could not be found at the indicated address." Sergei's wife, too, was then arrested. For Sedova the arrest of her son's wife was an act of "personal vengeance."

Then in early 1937 Trotsky disclosed another dimension to Sergei's arrest. The Soviet press was claiming that Sergei's family name was Bronstein and not Sedov, to emphasize "its Jewish sound," as Trotsky noted. "My son is accused, not more nor less, of an attempt to exterminate workers. Is this really so far from the accusation against the Jews of using Christian blood?" As Trotsky knew all too well, Stalin had used antisemitism as part of his struggle for power against the Opposition. The arrest of Sergei provided another cynical occasion.

By February 1937 Sergei's whereabouts were still unknown. In an open letter addressed "To the Conscience of the World," Sedova said that Sergei had been "arrested along with thousands of others, . . . spent eight months in a Moscow prison, and then was sent to Krasnoyarsk," where he was allowed to work in a factory. But this apparent compromise lent itself to a subterfuge, for it was in Krasnoyarsk that he was accused of "preparing a mass poisoning of workers." In despair, Sedova made her public appeal for support. But Stalin would not be swayed. Whatever they suspected, Sergei's parents never learned the truth about his fate: he was executed on October 29, 1937, with a bullet to the back of his skull.

Trotsky's stay in France was never entirely secure. Pressure to expel him came from Communist militants and right-wing officials. Following Kirov's murder, *L'Humanité*, the organ of the French Communist Party, declared that "Trotsky's hands are covered with Kirov's blood." Trotsky feared that the shifting winds of internal French politics and diplomacy—the right-wing government of Edouard Daladier and Pierre Laval concluded an alliance with the Kremlin in the spring of 1935— would lead to his being deported, possibly to the French island colony of Madagascar, since no other country was willing to accept him. In desperation, Trotsky asked for asylum in Norway, where a Social Democratic government had just come into power. After many appeals, Trotsky was granted a visa.

He reached Norway on June 18, 1935, and quickly faced restrictions similar to those he had suffered in France. Given his notoriety, he could not find a suitable place to rent. It took a socialist editor, Konrad Knudsen, to offer him a quiet haven in his own home, in a small village thirty miles north of Oslo. As often happened, the tense uncertainties of Trotsky's life undermined his health. He was sick all summer and by October had to be hospitalized for six weeks to recover from severe fatigue.

Only then could Trotsky resume his writing; within a year he completed *The Revolution Betrayed*, his outspoken analysis of the Soviet Union at the height of Stalin's dictatorship. Like much of Trotsky's writings about the regime, *The Revolution Betrayed* expressed many mixed feelings and ideas. Trotsky defended collectivization, calling it "a truly gigantic revolution in socialized agriculture." He lauded "the unprecedented tempo of Russia's industrial development. . . . Socialism," he wrote, "has demonstrated its right to victory . . . not in the language of dialectics, but in the language of steel, cement, and electricity." But Trotsky also denounced the Kremlin's arbitrary violence. Perhaps he was thinking of his son, Sergei, when he wrote that many young people "who are outstanding and unsubmissive . . . are systematically destroyed, suppressed or physically exterminated." This is a "totalitarian regime of fear, lies, and flattery" which relies on concentration camps, isolation cells, and Siberian exile to intimidate the opposition and the broader population. He could not help concluding that Stalinism and fascism had a "deadly similarity." Very few

LEON TROTSKY

people at the time were willing to recognize the truth behind Trotsky's perceptive remark.

For Trotsky, there were two fundamental reasons behind this tragedy. Lenin had not foreseen Russia's prolonged isolation after the first proletarian revolution had taken place. Revolutions failed to break out in Europe, leaving Russia vulnerable and alone: vulnerable to Stalin's reliance on an entrenched, ruthless bureaucracy and alone among hostile capitalist states bent on strangling her. Lenin's idea remained alive, as proved by the country's unprecedented economic development guided by centralized planning; it was Stalin who had betrayed it. Trotsky could take heart only from his firm belief that the country's economic advances and the state's control of factories and natural resources would someday overcome the consequences of Stalin's personal dictatorship.

Trotsky was in Norway when events in Madrid and Moscow erupted onto the world stage. In July 1936 the Spanish military, led by General Francisco Franco, rebelled against the government; this was the beginning of the Spanish Civil War. And on August 5 the first of the three notorious "show trials" began in Moscow. Sixteen defendants, among them Lev Kamenev and Grigory Zinoviev, were charged with high treason, conspiracy, and attempts to assassinate Stalin. The indictment went on to claim that Trotsky, assisted by his son Lev, was at the center of the terrorist plot. The principal charge was the establishment of a "Trotskyite-Zinovievite Terrorist Center," which was held responsible for the assassination of Kirov. For five days, the defendants—taking on the role of repentant traitors—confessed to implausible crimes. Zinoviev, once among the closest of Lenin's colleagues, declared that he was "second only to Trotsky" in organizing a plot to kill Stalin, Voroshilov, and other leaders. "My defective Bolshevism became transformed into anti-Bolshevism and through Trotskyism I arrived at fascism.

Trotskyism," Zinoviev concluded, "is a variety of fascism." Another defendant, Ivan Smirnov, who had been a close colleague of Trotsky and had organized the defeat of Admiral Kolchak in the Civil War, claimed that Trotsky had been sending "directives and instructions on terrorism and regards our state as a fascist state. . . . He is on the other side of the barricades."

Trotsky tried to grasp what was happening. By the second day, he began to issue statements: he offered to submit himself to a Commission on Political Terrorism sponsored by the League of Nations, even to accept extradition to Moscow if an independent commission found him guilty of the crimes alleged against him by the Kremlin. He compared the trial to Edgar Allan Poe's story "The Pit and the Pendulum." "Human nerves," he wrote, "even the strongest, have a limited capacity to endure moral torture." Soviet authorities pressed for his expulsion from Norway on the grounds that Oslo should not be granting refuge to such a notorious criminal. They did not, however, ask for extradition on the basis of the trial's indictment because that would mean an impartial hearing before a Norwegian judge.

Although Oslo officials resisted expelling him, they grew increasingly restive with Trotsky in their midst. The Norwegian minister of justice at the time was Trygve Lie, who later became the first secretary general of the United Nations. Under pressure from the Kremlin and from Nazi sympathizers, Lie ordered the internment of Trotsky and his wife. They were forcibly taken from Knudsen's home and placed under house arrest, guarded by twenty policemen. Their mail was censored and they were not permitted to receive newspapers. All this served Stalin's purposes. In the wake of the first purge trial, Trotsky was now under severe public attack by the Kremlin and its supporters. But he could barely respond; for more than three months he and his wife endured an arbitrary confinement. His only solace was a short book that Lev produced in

Paris—with the assistance of Victor Serge, who had recently been released from exile and allowed to leave for France— which exposed the trial's factual inconsistencies, among them the prosecution's claim that Lev had met and conspired with his father at the Hotel Bristol in Copenhagen in November 1932; the hotel had been demolished in 1917, and Lev had never set foot in Copenhagen.

Norwegian officials remained adamant, caving in to pressure from the Kremlin and local pro-German activists. They insisted that Trotsky had violated the terms of his visit when he commented on political affairs in various countries. At one point, Trotsky lost his patience and denounced Trygve Lie in words that would prove prophetic. "This is your first act of surrender to Nazism in your own country. You will pay for this," Trotsky declared for all to hear. "You think yourselves secure and free to deal with a political exile as you please. But the day is near—remember this!—the day is near when the Nazis will drive you from your country." Four years later, after the Germans had captured Oslo, Lie and other ministers, joined by the elderly King Haakon, waited by the coast for a boat to take them to England. It was then that the king reminded them of "Trotsky's curse."

No country appeared ready to welcome him. Governments were wary of accepting such a notorious revolutionary, and many liberal figures, who might otherwise have been sympathetic, hesitated to voice their support. Earlier that year, Hitler had dispatched German troops into the Rhineland, a direct violation of the Versailles Treaty, which had called for the region's demilitarization; neither France nor England moved to enforce the treaty and challenge Hitler's first military move. All these developments worked in Stalin's favor; with the rise of Nazism, many people were hesitant to criticize Soviet policies in a world increasingly divided between loyalty to Stalin or to Hitler. Trotsky was trapped in the middle.

He was saved by a pair of unlikely angels. The artists Diego Rivera and his wife, Frida Kahlo, successfully petitioned the government of Mexico, led by President Lazaro Cardenas, to grant Trotsky a visa.* Trygve Lie informed him of this news on December 18; the following day Lie dispatched Trotsky and his wife across the Atlantic on an oil tanker. Along with a guard, they were the only passengers. The ship arrived on the Mexican coast on January 9, 1937. Kahlo was on hand to greet them, joined by Mexican officials and Trotsky's American follower Max Shachtman. Trotsky and Sedova were taken on the presidential train to Mexico City, where Rivera and Kahlo offered them the hospitality of their home in the suburb of Coyoacán. The climate, the stunning landscapes, the open, relaxed reception by Mexican officials gave them a feeling of genuine renewal. "We were breathing purified air," Sedova wrote to friends. "A motorcar took us to the train; . . . it carried us across the fields of palms and cacti to the suburbs of Mexico City; a blue house, a patio filled with plants, airy rooms, collections of pre-Columbian art, paintings from all over: we were on a new planet, in Rivera's house." They lived there for two years. But Trotsky had no inclination to relax. He was restless. After months of house arrest in Norway, he had the run of the Blue House with its spacious courtyard. The American writer Eleanor Clark used to see him walking "back and forth, back and forth, like a lion in the zoo."† As he had done in Turkey, he quickly assembled a staff of translators and stenographers. American supporters recruited volunteers to serve as guards. Two weeks after his arrival, on January 23, the second show trial opened in Moscow.

*Rivera had been expelled from the Mexican Communist Party in 1929 as part of a broad, often indiscriminate purge engineered from Moscow; he then declared himself a Trotskyist.
†In 1937 Eleanor Clark spent several months in the Trotsky household, where she served as a translator; she was eighteen years old at the time. She later recalled her days with Trotsky in her novel *Gloria Mundi* (1979).

Its defendants included party figures who had once been among his closest allies: men like Karl Radek, Yury Pyatakov, and Christian Rakovsky. Now they turned against him. They accused Trotsky of planning to sabotage industry and to dismember the Soviet Union for the purpose of parceling out the pieces to Nazi Germany and Imperial Japan; to accomplish all this they claimed that he had met secretly with Hitler's aide Rudolf Hess. This time both of his sons were implicated: Lev was his father's principal henchman, while Sergei was attempting to poison workers.

Based in Mexico and with direct access to the American and international press, Trotsky threw himself into a rush of activity, issuing statements and sending myriad instructions to Lev in Paris and supporters in New York. He insisted on receiving clippings from old Soviet newspapers and other material to disprove the Kremlin's claims. It turned out to be easy to refute several self-incriminating claims of the defendants. Pyatakov, for example, claimed that he had flown from Berlin to Oslo in December 1935 with the sole purpose of seeing Trotsky to pursue their conspiracy. But Trotsky confirmed that not a single foreign airplane had landed in Oslo that entire month, a testament to the rudimentary nature of commercial aviation during those European winters. So "Pyatakov was forced by the GPU to fly to see me in an imaginary airplane just as the Holy Inquisition forced witches to go to their rendezvous with the devil on a broomstick," Trotsky wrote. "All the other confessions, especially insofar as they concern me," he insisted, "are built upon the same miserable subterfuges and falsifications." But Stalin "cannot stop. He resembles a man who drinks a salt solution to quench his thirst."

Trotsky also pointed out the antisemitic dimension to the trials, in particular that the Soviet press had highlighted the original family names of Kamenev and Zinoviev—Rozenfeld and Radomyslsky. In New York, the Yiddish journalist B. Z.

Goldberg responded with anger. "The very fact that [Trotsky] has suddenly discovered Jews with a Jewish question, with Yiddish and even with a Jewish territory, seems to me weird. . . . In order to beat Stalin, Trotsky considers it right to make Soviet Russia antisemitic. . . . For us this is a very serious matter. . . . We are accustomed to look to the Soviet Union as our sole consolation as far as antisemitism is concerned." Even Rabbi Stephen Wise, the most famous American rabbi of his generation, regarded Trotsky's claim of antisemitism against Stalin as a "cowardly device." But Trotsky did not back down. In the face of often hostile remarks from Western apologists for the Soviet regime, he called for the establishment of an impartial international commission to review the evidence, seeking "people who incontestably enjoy authority and public confidence."

The Moscow trials, the increasing tensions in Europe, Trotsky's unexpected presence in Mexico, and his eloquent pleas of innocence exacerbated the confusion among many liberal and radical figures in America who were already conflicted over the decade's political and ideological dilemmas. For many intellectuals, the Great Depression and the triumphs of Hitler and Mussolini sapped their confidence in democracy, a confidence that the Roosevelt administration, for all its dynamic energy, could not restore. Living in Mexico, Trotsky was able to follow their debates in left-wing journals. It was not an easy relationship in either direction. Trotsky had little patience for reform-minded liberals, while radicals in New York, who wanted to regard Trotsky as one of their own, had difficulty realizing that, unlike themselves, he was a genuine revolutionary.

Two American weeklies—the *Nation* and the *New Republic*—got under his skin with their credulous reaction to the Moscow trials. In an editorial in February 1937, the *New Republic* asked, "What do we actually know about the trials?" Since the defendants had "fully confessed their guilt on all counts," there seemed little reason to question the integrity of the proceedings. Malcolm Cowley, who became literary editor of the *New Republic* in 1931 and was one of the most admired critics in America, was not above crass apologetics when it came to the trials. For Cowley, "The liberals who get caught up in the controversy on moral grounds are stooges and suckers." Taking the indictment and the confessions at face value, Cowley wrote a long review of the transcript of the second trial that was issued within weeks after its conclusion. He observed in the *New Republic* in April 1937, "The confessions were undoubtedly sincere"; the trials confirmed "the scrupulousness and good faith of the Soviet authorities"; and Trotsky's

> hatred of Stalin made him go too fast for those who accepted his leadership; it involved them in conspiracies and murders and acts of sabotage; it separated them from the masses. And Trotsky's self-centeredness, his lack of personal loyalties, made him disown the Russian Trotskyists just as soon as they were discovered and arrested. . . . It was not the great leader who was betrayed by his followers: it was the followers who were betrayed and hurried to their deaths by the great leader.

As for the Soviet Union, "it is still the most progressive force in the world."

The *Nation*'s reporting was equally tendentious. In the wake of the initial show trial in August 1936, an editorial claimed, "There can be no doubt that dictatorship in Russia is dying and that a new democracy is being born." In the same issue, Louis Fischer, who had spent years in Moscow, reviewed the new Soviet Constitution. For Fischer, "ruthlessness and terror had ceased to be the state's most trusted weapon. . . . The world has seen a number of parliamentary regimes converted into dictatorships. The Bolshevik dictatorship is the first to resign in favor of democracy." Later, in January 1937, the *Nation* continued its naive, if not willfully misinforming, commentary. It cited the reports by Walter Duranty in the *New*

York Times as reason to fully accept the defendants' confessions. "It would have been possible for Radek to say a few words of repudiation in open court in the presence of foreign correspondents and the diplomatic corps, and with those words to electrify the whole world," one editorial imagined. "That he did not do so carries considerable conviction."

Angered by such pieces, Trotsky refused to countenance a visit by Freda Kirchwey, the editor of the *Nation*. As he wrote to Herbert Solow in February 1937, "I cannot discuss personally with a man or woman who has doubts about my not being an ally of Hitler and the Mikado. I give her full authorization to suffer these doubts in her own home, but not in mine." Trotsky was determined to "break the state of neutrality in regard to the *Nation* and the *New Republic*," to "destroy their influence on radical thought." Their editors were "bombastic, pretentious and hypocritical" and "stand in the way of every movement forward."

Given what we know today, it is nearly impossible to put ourselves in the frame of mind that prevailed among certain intellectual circles in the West. Otherwise intelligent and critically minded writers and professors were so mesmerized by Stalin's Russia that they accepted outrageous accusations against men who had been among Lenin's closest collaborators: that they had wanted to assassinate Lenin and Stalin, to betray the country to Germany and Japan, to sabotage industry, derail trains, poison workers. Trotsky had to defend them all, even those, like Kamenev and Zinoviev, who had once conspired against him.

Just months after he reached Mexico, Trotsky was in correspondence with the founders of *Partisan Review*, an antistalinist journal that hoped to counter the influence of apologists for the Kremlin. He initially welcomed the new journal and accepted an invitation to contribute, hoping it would be "pitilessly directed against the ideological poisons of both the Second and Third Internationals, poisons which are no less harmful in the sphere of culture, science, and art than in the sphere of economics and politics." But he soon understood that the journal's mix of political commentary and literary reviews was not to his taste. As he wrote to the critic Dwight MacDonald in January 1938, "It is my general impression that the editors of *Partisan Review* are capable, educated and intelligent people but *they have nothing to say*." Invited to participate in a symposium on Marxism, Trotsky saw no utility in contributing. "Some of [the contributors] are political corpses. How can a corpse be entrusted with deciding whether Marxism is a living force?"

Trotsky also corresponded with the critic Philip Rahv, who, like MacDonald, was an editor at *Partisan Review*. Trotsky recognized that the journal was independent of the Stalinist cast of mind. "But independence alone is not sufficient," he warned Rahv.

> Certain measures are necessary for the struggle against incorrect theory; other measures for the struggle against epidemic cholera. Stalinism is infinitely nearer to cholera than to false theory. The struggle must be intense, truculent, merciless. An element of "fanaticism" in this struggle is not only valid but salutary. We will leave it to the Philistines to ridicule "fanaticism." Nothing great has been accomplished in history without fanaticism.

The controversy over the trials provoked strenuous arguments. The philosopher Sidney Hook, who had once been a convinced Marxist, campaigned to refute the charges against Trotsky out of respect for the truth. In February 1937 Hook wrote to Albert Einstein at Princeton, asking for support of an international commission to examine the allegations. Einstein readily agreed that "every accused person should be given an opportunity to establish his innocence," but he did not see how a public hearing could help Trotsky. When Hook persisted, even visiting Einstein to press his case, Einstein refused to endorse an appeal; he could only observe that "both Stalin and Trotsky are political gangsters."

But Trotsky's call for a commission of inquiry did not go unheeded. In March 1937 a delegation of Americans and Europeans under the leadership of the philosopher John Dewey arrived in Mexico to interview Trotsky and examine his material.* The commission met in Rivera and Kahlo's Blue House in the suburb of Coyoacán where they took testimony for the better part of a week. Trotsky's testimony concluded the hearing. He spoke to the commissioners for almost four hours in flawed and halting English, determined to make up for his lack of fluency by speaking in a language they understood. He had prepared meticulously, relying on Lev in Paris to track down endless numbers of articles to prove the falseness of Stalin's accusations. Throughout the week, Dewey and Trotsky had kept their distance from each other, mostly to safeguard the objectivity of the hearings. But once Trotsky's testimony was over, they had a chance to talk and expressed their mutual respect. Albert Glotzer, an American who worked closely with Trotsky in Mexico and made a shorthand transcript of the proceedings, saw the men sitting together at a party later that same evening. As he reported, Dewey remarked to Trotsky, "If all Communists were like you, I would be a Communist." And Trotsky, equally gracious, responded, "If all liberals were like you, I would be a liberal." The Dewey commission issued its report later in the year, declaring the Moscow trials to be nothing more than "a frame-up" and Trotsky to be innocent of the charges against him. Dewey was well known in America, assur-

---

*Sidney Hook had prevailed on Dewey to accept leadership of the commission. Dewey and the other participants were subjected to myriad threats and appeals by American Stalinists, urging them to resign from the committee. Dewey was also offered a tour of the Soviet Union to see for himself how wonderful things were, an offer he dismissed out of hand.

ing news coverage of the commission's report. But in Europe, tensions over Germany's resurgence were preoccupying the press; little was said about the Dewey commission. By then, as well, the ideological certainties of the era made it difficult for the Dewey commission's long report, with its unequivocal declaration of Trotsky's innocence, to persuade the unpersuadable.

That same spring of 1937, in the midst of his frenetic activity, Trotsky indulged in a brief affair with Frida Kahlo. It was a reckless adventure. Though Kahlo and Rivera were not famous for their fidelity, Rivera had a ferocious sense of jealousy; had he known of the liaison, he probably would have thrown Trotsky out—if he did not shoot him first. Such a rupture would have made political difficulties for Trotsky in Mexico, as his staff felt compelled to remind him. The affair with Kahlo caused a breach in Trotsky and Sedova's relationship. He had pursued other women before, but now he and his wife had experienced the full range of emotional despair together— political downfall, exile, the loss of his daughters, the disappearance of their younger son. At one point in July, Trotsky went off on his own, staying in a small hotel, all the while sending Sedova frequent letters expressing his chagrin and devotion. One letter was a playful and passionate expression of his love for her in graphic, erotic detail. In other letters and telephone calls—perhaps out of shame for his behavior and a desire to embarrass her over what might have been an episode of infidelity of her own—he reminded Sedova that a younger man had pursued her in 1918 when they were living in the Kremlin. It was all Sedova could do to deflect his continuing jealousy. They reconciled and resumed socializing with Rivera and Kahlo, enjoying picnics together as if nothing had happened.

Lev continued to be his father's closest collaborator. In Paris, his job was to produce the *Bulletin of the Opposition*, to sustain contact with a host of supporters, and to carry out faithfully his father's numerous and insistent assignments. The Kremlin was aware of Lev's role and devised a way to compromise his work, dispatching a Russian émigré named Mark Zborowski to insinuate himself into Lev's circle of supporters. By the fall of 1936 Zborowski came to assume major responsibilities: working with Lev on the *Bulletin*, facilitating correspondence, maintaining files of material connected to the Opposition. Zborowski undoubtedly engineered the theft of Trotsky's archive in Paris in November 1936, when 190 pounds of files were stolen. This was not the first time the Kremlin succeeded in infiltrating Trotsky's circle. It is now known that several bodyguards Trotsky had accepted in Turkey were Kremlin agents, assigned to monitor him closely but to do him no harm.

Over the winter of 1937–1938, Lev began to feel unwell. He was under tremendous pressure: from his father to work incessantly, from complications in his private life, from continuous lack of funds—he once complained to Trotsky that he sometimes did "not even have the money to buy postage stamps"—and from the broader political tensions of the era. In February his doctors, suspecting appendicitis, urged him to undergo abdominal surgery. Using a pseudonym, he entered a small, private clinic whose staff included Russian émigrés. The surgery went normally and Lev appeared to be recovering, but after several days he experienced excruciating pain and was found stumbling through the halls, shouting incomprehensibly and foaming at the mouth. Doctors tried to assist him, but he soon succumbed.

Diego Rivera heard the news on the radio and rushed to locate Trotsky, who was staying with friends in another suburb. Once Rivera broke the news, Trotsky hurried back to Coyoacán to tell his wife. The death of Lev Sedov was a crushing blow. His daughters deceased, Sergei imprisoned and presumed dead, now all his children, all *their* children were gone. For Trotsky,

Lev's death had particular consequences. He had not been the easiest father or collaborator. All the awkward difficulties that others experienced, Lev had endured with even greater intensity. Trotsky did not spare himself, was exacting in his demands on others, and was only grudgingly generous with his praise. As Eleanor Clark saw for herself, "Any inconvenience for him was a setback for the world." He frequently berated Lev about problems with the editing and printing of the *Bulletin*, about tardy distribution. In February 1937, when Trotsky was gathering material about the second Moscow trial, he sent a letter telling Lev that his work was so slovenly it bordered "on treachery," then went on to allege, "It is difficult to say which are the worst blows, those from Moscow or those from Paris." And in January 1938, as Trotsky impatiently waited for an issue of the *Bulletin* with its coverage of the Dewey commission report, he berated Lev, calling his handling of the *Bulletin* an "outright crime" and threatening to move the editorial office to New York.

Overcome with grief, Trotsky and Sedova secluded themselves; they barely emerged from their room for a week. Trotsky, though, did not surrender. He soon prepared a heartfelt tribute to Lev in which he acknowledged the strains in their relationship and the dangers Lev endured in Paris. He insisted that Kremlin agents were responsible for his death, "whether the Moscow masters resorted to chemistry, or whether everything they had previously done proved sufficient." As for him and his wife, he made clear the magnitude of their despair: "Together with our boy has died everything that still remained young within us." Determined to expose a presumed conspiracy, he demanded a full investigation. French doctors reported that they could find no evidence that Lev had been poisoned or that his medical treatment had been maliciously compromised. Trotsky believed otherwise and pressed hard through lawyers and political supporters for further investigations. By the mid-

1950s, a partial confession by Zborowski himself helped Western scholars confirm that he had been a Stalinist agent, who could well have had the means to murder Lev or to arrange his death. Lev had been his father's most important political collaborator. No doubt Stalin wanted him out of the way; there is some evidence that agents were seeking to kidnap Lev in order to bring him back to Moscow, where he would be tried and condemned. In any case, no one has been able to confirm exactly what happened to Lev Sedov during those days in February 1938.

Stalin's bloodlust was not easy to assuage. As he once remarked to a colleague, "The greatest delight is to mark one's enemy, prepare everything, avenge oneself thoroughly, and then go to sleep." In addition to Trotsky's two daughters and two sons, whose deaths were either directly or indirectly caused by Stalin, a host of relatives faced imprisonment or execution: his first wife,* an older brother, a younger sister, a niece, three nephews, and three sons-in-law were all shot; still other nieces and nephews and one granddaughter endured prison and exile; the fate of two grandchildren from his daughter Nina and his grandson from his son Lev is unknown. It was as if someone had assembled Trotsky's family tree, then systematically denuded the leaves. Others who had worked closely with him were also targeted. Erwin Wolf had worked for Trotsky in Norway; he made his way in 1936 to Spain, where he was killed by Stalinist agents. Rudolf Klement, a German émigré who had served Trotsky as his secretary in

---

*Although Trotsky had left Sokolovskaya and their two infant daughters in Siberia when he first escaped in 1902, she remained loyal to him to the end. As late as August 1935, when he was in France, she wrote him about the difficult conditions that family members were enduring. She then thanked him for providing some material support for her: "I am very touched, as always, by your thoughtful attitude toward me." She was later sent to Siberia and executed in 1938.

France and then as secretary of the Fourth International, was kidnapped and murdered in Paris in the summer of 1938; his mutilated body was found in the Seine.

Following the death of Zinaida in Berlin, her son Seva was looked after by his uncle Lev, who arranged homes and orphanages for him to live in. But after Lev's death, Seva was taken in by Lev's longtime companion Jeanne Martin Molinier, who had broken with the main group of Trotsky's followers. It required the strenuous efforts of activists and friends of Trotsky to secure control of Seva and arrange his travel to Mexico, where he joined his grandparents in August 1939; by then, he was thirteen years old. Trotsky had once expressed concern that Seva was forgetting his Russian while he learned French and German in European schools. But after the boy reached Mexico, Trotsky understood that Seva should have the chance to enjoy a normal life. He instructed the entire household, including Sedova and the bodyguards, never to speak to Seva in Russian and never to discuss politics with him. Under the name Esteban Volkov, he grew up in Mexico City, attended a private school founded by Spanish refugees, studied chemistry, and became a researcher in the pharmaceutical industry; he married and raised four daughters.

As the purge trials unfolded in Moscow, thoughtful figures on the left began to reexamine their understanding of Stalinism and its origins in Lenin's own extreme measures. Inevitably this led to questions about Trotsky's exercise of power. Several of his critics, among them the anarchist Emma Goldman, pointed to his role in suppressing the Kronstadt rebellion in 1921. "It does not occur to [Trotsky]," Goldman wrote, "that one might detest the savage in the Kremlin and his cruel regime and yet not exonerate Leon Trotsky from the crime against the sailors of Kronstadt." Goldman refused to see any significant difference between Stalin and Trotsky. Stalin "did not come down as a gift from heaven to the hapless Russian people," she insisted. "He is merely continuing the Bolshevik traditions, even if in a more relentless manner."

Another critic was the writer Victor Serge, one of a handful of followers who had the courage to challenge Trotsky. Born in Belgium, Serge had joined the Bolshevik cause in Petrograd in 1919. But after supporting Trotsky in the 1920s, he fell victim to Stalin's repressions and was arrested in 1933, then sent into exile in Orenburg. Supporters in the West rallied to his defense; their efforts gained his release in 1936 and he was allowed to leave for Paris. Serge quickly established contact with Lev Sedov and began a correspondence with Trotsky in Mexico. But Serge soon came to understand that the opposition to Stalin was suffused with ideological intolerance when it needed to advocate political liberty. In *Memoirs of a Revolutionary*, Serge explained how he had implored Trotsky to "include in the Opposition's program a declaration of freedom for all parties accepting the Soviet system. . . . The only problem which revolutionary Russia, in all the years from 1917 to 1923, utterly failed to consider was the problem of liberty, the only declaration which it had to make afresh and which it never made is the Declaration of the Rights of Man."

In one of their exchanges in April 1936, shortly after Serge reached Paris, Trotsky expressed his long-standing hostility to the Mensheviks, the onetime allies of the Bolsheviks in the Social Democratic movement; they had broken with Lenin in 1917 over the question of one-party rule. Nonetheless, many of their cadres fought alongside the Bolsheviks against White forces during the Civil War. In subsequent years, they faced repression from both Lenin and Stalin. Yet Trotsky sustained his animus toward them. Asked what the policy of the Fourth International would be toward the Mensheviks should it ever gain power, Trotsky did not hesitate to offer a cynical response. "If the adherents of the Mensheviks would imprison and kill new Liebknechts [the German Communist Karl Liebknecht had been murdered alongside Rosa Luxemburg in Berlin in 1919], then we, of course, would not pat the Mensheviks on the head." But the Mensheviks were not responsible for the murder of the German Communist leaders, and few of them had joined the Whites during the Civil War. This was nothing more than a demagogic response on Trotsky's part.*

He rejected Serge's criticism and broke off relations with him. But Serge was equally firm. In his memoirs, he wrote:

> I came to the conclusion that our Opposition had simultaneously contained two opposite lines of significance. For the great majority of its members it had meant resistance to totalitarianism in the name of the democratic ideals expressed at the beginning of the Revolution; for a number of our old Bolshevik leaders it meant on the contrary the defense of doctrinal orthodoxy which, while not excluding a certain tendency toward democracy, was authoritarian through and through. . . . If [Trotsky] in his exile from the U.S.S.R. . . . had made himself the ideologist of a renewed socialism, critical in outlook and fearing diversity less than dogmatism, perhaps he would have attained a new greatness. But he was the prisoner of his own orthodoxy, the more so since the lapses into unorthodoxy were being denounced as treason. He saw his role as that of one carrying into the world at large a movement which was not only Russian but extinct in Russia itself, killed twice over, both by the bullets of its executioners and by changes in human mentality.

---

*Trotsky in exile sustained his antagonism toward the Mensheviks. This led him to a grievous error in judgment in 1931, when he condemned several leading Mensheviks during their trial in Moscow. Accused of sabotage and conspiring with their émigré colleagues against Stalin's regime, they were convicted on the basis of confessions and falsified evidence, much in the way the later show trials employed similar methods. Five years later, Trotsky publicly expressed his regret over this decision.

In response to critics, Trotsky wrote *Their Morals and Ours*, a pamphlet he issued in early 1938 (and dedicated to the memory of Lev Sedov). It echoed his ideas from 1919, when he defended the Bolsheviks' monopoly of power and resort to revolutionary terror. He again offered a broad defense of coercion in the service of political ideas as long as they were the most commendable in his eyes. "A means can be justified only by its end," he wrote. "But the end in turn needs to be justified. From the Marxist point of view, which expresses the historical interests of the proletariat, the end is justified if it leads to increasing the power of man over nature and to the abolition of the power of man over man." For Trotsky it was a matter of faith that class struggle was the only way to achieve universal freedom. Virtually any means, as long they were sincerely designed to further class struggle, could be justified. He remained, after all the tragedy and suffering that had touched his family, and after all the millions who had been destroyed by the revolution he had championed, a firm defender of the Bolshevik seizure of power and an opponent of orderly, parliamentary democracy based on respect for civil liberties and minority rights. He remained convinced that justice could be established by means of a dictatorship, or at least the kind of dictatorship he had in mind. And he continued to refuse any moral responsibility for the loss of innocent life he and his ideas had caused.

John Dewey felt the urge to respond to *Their Morals and Ours*. He knew and admired Trotsky, but he grasped the logical fallacy at the heart of Trotsky's argument.

> The selection of class struggle as a means has to be justified, on the ground of the interdependence of means and end, by an examination of actual consequences of its use. . . . That it is such a means has to be shown not by "deduction" from a law but by examination of the actual relations of means and

consequences; an examination in which, given the liberation of mankind as end, there is free and unprejudiced search for the means by which it can be attained.

But that was not how Trotsky saw things. His belief in class struggle had more in common with theological certainty, with the kind of faith that characterized religious belief, than with a scrupulous regard for scientific or historical examination. Although Dewey's essay disappointed him, he did not respond in print.

George Orwell also weighed in. Writing in 1939, he was well aware of Trotsky's opposition to Stalin, but did not succumb to Trotsky's allure. "He is probably as much responsible for [the Russian dictatorship] as any man now living, and there is no certainty that as a dictator he would be preferable to Stalin, though undoubtedly he has a much more interesting mind. The essential act," Orwell concluded, "is the rejection of democracy—that is, of the underlying values of democracy; once you have decided upon that, Stalin—or at any rate someone *like* Stalin—is already on the way."

Emma Goldman, Victor Serge, John Dewey, George Orwell—each was a firm opponent of Stalinism and each, in spite of regard for Trotsky's courage, parted company with him over questions of morality and democracy. As Serge saw for himself, Trotsky was "a prisoner of his own orthodoxy."

But Trotsky's devotion to Marxism-Leninism posed one difficult challenge for him: whether or not to remain at least formally an adherent of the Third International. This was Lenin's creation, an initiative he took in 1919 to supersede the Second International, which had been a coalition of Socialist parties. The Third International, or the Comintern, was intended to mobilize revolutionary Communist Parties in Europe to follow the lead of the successful Bolsheviks. After the triumph of Hitler in Germany, Trotsky and his followers referred to themselves as members of a Fourth International, but it was only formally established in September 1938 with a meeting in France attended by twenty-one delegates. Trotsky often expressed great hopes in this new coalition. In a letter to Victor Serge in April 1938, Trotsky insisted that "only the Fourth International will be a revolutionary factor in the nearest future." And in October, when he addressed a meeting of his followers in New York via a recording of his speech, Trotsky assured his audience, "During the next ten years the program of the Fourth International will become the guide of millions and those revolutionary millions will know how to storm earth and heaven." But it was not to be; his misplaced optimism could not obscure the fact that the Fourth International, divided among rival ideological claims and infiltrated by Stalinist agents, never attracted more than a few thousand followers and posed no substantial threat to the political order in Europe or North America.

As Germany rearmed and Franco gained the advantage in Spain, Trotsky grasped the likely complexities of the conflict to come. "Each day the press peers out toward the world horizon, looking for smoke and flames," he wrote in his essay "On the Threshold of a New World War." "There will be shooting, but who will shoot at whom, nobody knows." As smaller states clamored for peace, their gestures resembled "a puppet show on the crater of a volcano." And while Soviet diplomacy pressed for a security agreement with England and France, Trotsky foresaw the likelihood, as early as August 1937—two years before the Molotov-Ribbentrop Pact—that if such an agreement were to fall through, "a union of Hitler with Stalin will not only become a possibility but an inevitability." But in case of war, the Soviet Union must be defended. It remained a workers' state because the means of production remained in the hands of the people, as if, for Trotsky, this fact alone defined socialism.

With war likely, the fate of the Jews intruded on his consciousness. In February 1932 Trotsky wrote to an editor in
New York that he was "against Zionism and all other aspects of
self-isolation on the part of the Jewish workers." In late 1933
Trotsky told the *New York Times* that he viewed Hitler's persecution of the Jews as a way to distract the population from the
country's social problems. But he knew that he had not studied
the "Jewish Question" adequately.* Five years later, in September 1938, with the situation in Germany even more acute,
Trotsky urged his followers in the Fourth International to confront antisemitism. "Before exhausting or drowning mankind
in blood, capitalism befouls the world atmosphere with the
poisonous vapors of national and race hatred. Antisemitism
today is one of the more malignant convulsions of capitalism's
death agony." Three months later, in the wake of Kristallnacht,
Trotsky's fears grew more urgent. "The number of countries
which expel Jews grows without cease. The number of countries able to accept them decreases," he wrote in "The Jewish
Bourgeoisie and Revolutionary Struggle." "It is possible to
imagine without difficulty what awaits the Jews at the mere
outbreak of the future world war. But even without war the
next development of world reaction signifies almost with certainty the *physical extermination of the Jews.*" He could not imagine an alternative. The idea of settling in Palestine was "a tragic
mirage." Birobidjan, the Soviet Jewish autonomous district near
the border with China, was "a bureaucratic nightmare." He expressed both profound anxiety over the fate of the Jews and obtuse ideological prescriptions of what they should do. "Now
more than ever, the fate of the Jewish people—not only their

---

*In a letter to Herbert Solow on January 29, 1934, Trotsky wrote that
"the 'Jewish Question' is now taking on new urgency. I am being asked from
all sides to say something about this issue. Unfortunately, I studied it very
little in the past." He wrote this letter soon after Hitler's accession to power.

political but also their physical fate—is indissolubly linked with the emancipating struggle of the international proletariat."

Only once, in January 1937, after he reached Mexico, when he responded to a series of questions from the New York *Forverts*, did Trotsky, mindful of the persecution of the Jews in Germany, back away from his long-held belief that they would assimilate within their countries of residence. Even under socialism, he now recognized, the Jews might well need a temporary territorial solution. But a close reading of the interview and other letters and statements makes clear that this was a grudging recognition of reality and not a profound shift in his thinking or consciousness of himself as a vulnerable Jew. He remained skeptical, if not antagonistic, to the idea of a Jewish homeland in Palestine.

Trotsky's friendship with Diego Rivera had survived the affair with Frida Kahlo. But by early 1939 their political differences and Rivera's own ambitions intruded. That year Rivera began to nurture contact with marginal anarchist and labor union groups that were antagonistic to Trotsky. He announced his resignation from the Fourth International and denounced Trotsky for not supporting a left-wing candidate to succeed President Cardenas when he would have to leave office. Rivera then founded a new party of his own.* Trotsky, who had pledged not to interfere in Mexico's internal affairs, concluded that he had to forgo Rivera's patronage and leave the Blue House. After some effort, his staff found a suitable new

---

*Rivera was hopelessly ignorant of politics. After World War II, he told a visiting young American activist that Trotsky had been killed on the orders of Hitler because, Rivera assured his listener, Stalin was about to summon Trotsky to Moscow, where he would assume leadership of the Red Army! I am grateful to Professor Hilary Putnam of Harvard for recounting his encounter with Rivera in Mexico City.

home, a compound several blocks away on Avenida Viena that could be cleaned and renovated within two months. Trotsky moved there in May, and it was from that address that he followed the outbreak of war in Europe.

After the Molotov-Ribbentrop Pact of August 1939, the Soviet Union occupied eastern Poland, then demanded from Estonia, Latvia, and Lithuania—which had gained their independence after World War I—the right to station military forces within their borders, a demand they could not resist. By the spring of 1940 Stalin had incorporated the three Baltic states into the Soviet Union. Trotsky refused to condemn these moves, convinced of the need to defend the Soviet Union come what may. In November 1939 the war reached into Finland when Stalin invaded, feeling the need to extend the defense network around Leningrad. But the Finns gamely resisted, exposing the Red Army's ineptitude and thereby encouraging Hitler. Soviet forces prevailed only after a hundred days of heavy fighting. Trotsky continued to defend Stalin's offensive, even claiming against all available evidence that the Red Army was intervening on behalf of an embattled Finnish proletariat. His tortuous reasoning bewildered followers in New York and elsewhere.

On the Western Front, French defenses collapsed in June 1940, allowing the Wehrmacht to occupy Paris. Trotsky understood that Germany's triumph undermined Stalin's strategy, which had depended on the French engaging Germany in a protracted war just as they had in World War I. Now Germany was not bogged down in the West. It was a catastrophe. Trotsky insisted on pointing out "the criminal and sinister role played by the Kremlin." Stalin had calculated that the Nonaggression Pact with Hitler would gain time to prepare for war, but he made a fundamental strategic error. By agreeing to the division of Poland, as Trotsky recognized, Stalin allowed the Polish buffer to disappear, giving Germany "a common frontier with the U.S.S.R." Now German "victories in the West are only preparation for a gigantic move toward the east." Stalin had wanted to avoid war, but this did not mean that "war will spare Stalin."

With grim news coming from Europe, Trotsky was able to employ his trenchant pen. He needed to earn money to sustain his household, with its many translators, typists, and guards; he had been paid well to write a biography of Stalin, but the manuscript was now more than a year behind schedule. It was getting harder for him to work. He suffered from high blood pressure and assumed he would die from a stroke. Doctors urged him to relax, to take naps in the afternoon. He would often start his day by feeding chickens and rabbits in the cages he had installed in the compound's courtyard. At other times, when he felt up to it, he traveled into the countryside for picnics or to search for unusual cactus plants, which he dug up and brought home.

In the final years of his life, Trotsky worked tirelessly to gain permission to go to the United States. America had fascinated him since his stay in 1917; he also believed he would be safer there. In the spring of 1938 he was in touch with his publisher, Cass Canfield of Harper and Brothers, looking for a way to work in New York, where he could get access to old newspapers. He approached followers like James Cannon to see about a visit to California. He appealed to Roger Baldwin, the leader of the American Civil Liberties Union. Nothing worked. In an interview with the *Daily News* in December 1938, Trotsky voiced his frustration over America's refusal to admit him. He had once gone to New York "without any passport, without any visa, without any absurd and humiliating formalities! Your immigration authorities were interested that I did not have trachoma but were absolutely unconcerned about my ideas." Now he sought a visa from an unlikely source.

Martin Dies was a reactionary congressman, a Democrat from Texas, who headed the House Un-American Activities Committee from 1938 to 1944. In the fall of 1939 his staff broached the idea of inviting Trotsky to testify about the history of Stalinism. Trotsky's followers argued against cooperating—his testimony would be perceived as an act of complicity with America's extreme right wing—but he was so eager to procure a visa for the United States, even a temporary one, that he did his best to accommodate the committee.* There was a plan to welcome Trotsky to Austin in October 1939. But Dies soon canceled the invitation, claiming that Mexico would not guarantee that Trotsky could return. Still, Trotsky and his staff continued to probe every possible avenue. He met discreetly with American consular officials in Mexico, offering to share sensitive information about the Mexican Communist Party and about Stalinist agents in America. Perhaps he was trying to make himself useful to American intelligence in order to gain a visa, or perhaps, given the pressures he was under, he believed that the more American agencies knew, the safer he would be.

Trotsky's contacts with the Dies Committee made it easier for Stalinists in Mexico to attack him. Under the Kremlin's directions, Trotsky had long been portrayed as an agent of Western imperialism; then with the rise of Hitler, Soviet propaganda linked him to fascism. His evident willingness to cooperate with the House committee gave Stalinists in Mexico another opening. They began to spread rumors that Trotsky would divulge information about Communist activities in Latin America and even discuss the Mexican oil industry, a sensitive issue within the country and with the United States. All this helped to compromise Trotsky in leftist circles, where a campaign to expel him from Mexico as an undesirable alien had waxed and waned ever since his arrival.

But Mexican Stalinists had a more sinister purpose in mind; they wanted him dead. Early in the morning of May 24,

---

*Freda Kirchwey of the *Nation* once called Dies a "One-man Gestapo from Texas."

1940, twenty well-armed men mounted a surprise assault on Trotsky's compound. Their leader was the Mexican artist David Siquieros. A convinced Stalinist, Siquieros had fought against Franco in the International Brigade, then returned to Mexico determined to serve the Kremlin. He assembled the attackers. Dressed in the uniforms of Mexican soldiers and police, they overpowered a five-man police unit that was assigned to guard Trotsky from a small house outside the walls of his compound; most were asleep and the attackers were able to subdue them without firing a shot. Aided by Robert Sheldon Harte, one of the American bodyguards who had recently come from New York, the attackers were given entry through the sliding garage door around 4 A.M., allowing them to secure the interior of the compound and keep the bodyguards in their own modest barrack. Determined to kill Trotsky, they sprayed automatic fire and threw incendiary bombs into the sleeping quarters. Sedova pushed Trotsky off the bed and lay on top of him. (Plagued by insomnia, he had taken sleeping pills earlier that night, which made it difficult for him to wake up.)

Seva, too, fell off his bed onto the floor, where he cowered in a corner. Even so, he was grazed in the ankle by a bullet that went through his mattress. An incendiary bomb ignited a fire in his bedroom, which was next to his grandparents'; Sedova had to smother it with a blanket. The attack lasted about fifteen minutes. The attackers fired more than three hundred bullets before they fled, taking both of Trotsky's cars. By the time the police and journalists arrived, Trotsky was ready to speak with them, and his spirited, boisterous attitude—he had just survived a murderous attack with only minor scratches from flying glass—left police officials suspecting that the shooting had been staged. The investigation soon confirmed that Harte was now missing, presumably kidnapped by the attackers. But as evidence mounted against Harte, Trotsky insisted on defending him, even after his body was found in a hideout. The attack compromised Trotsky's standing. The police remained suspicious that he had staged the attack himself to counter any pressure he was under to leave the country. They questioned members of the household and took two of Trotsky's guards into custody, hoping they would accuse him. The Communist press parroted the same story.

A week after the assault, Trotsky appealed to President Cardenas. He had survived an "enormous killing machine," while his grandson needed medical attention every day to heal the wound to his leg. But now the police were making "an unjust mistake," turning the victims "into the accused," he wrote. Cardenas intervened, ordering the release of Trotsky's men.

Determined to fend off another attack, Trotsky arranged increased security around the compound. No typing was allowed between 10 P.M. and 7 A.M. At night, the guards were to stay awake, carry fully loaded guns, and make their rounds every fifteen minutes. By June 22, the inventory of weapons included a shotgun, a Thompson submachine gun, and various rifles and pistols, including a .38-caliber Colt revolver for Trotsky and an automatic pistol for his wife. Five days later, they considered asking permission for additional weapons: twelve hand grenades, four automatic rifles, two submachine guns, four gas masks, and twenty luminous rockets. All this was designed to thwart the kind of attack they had just survived. Stalin, though, was planning something more devious.

In the fall of 1938 a Spaniard named Ramón Mercader, under the assumed name of Jacques Mornard, began to court a young, innocent, American follower of Trotsky named Sylvia Ageloff. They were introduced in Paris by a friend of Sylvia's who was part of a conspiracy to penetrate Trotsky's household. Her sister, Ruth Ageloff, was an occasional assistant to Trotsky in Mexico, where she served as a typist, translator, and researcher. Mornard claimed to be a businessman of Belgian origin. In reality, he was of Spanish and Cuban descent and had fought against Franco in the Civil War.* As their relationship grew more intimate, he nurtured her confidence and by 1940 was accompanying her to Mexico, where she visited her sister in the Trotsky compound. By then, Mornard had entered North America with a false passport under the name of Frank Jacson; Sylvia, ever gullible, accepted his explanation that he needed to assume another identity in order to avoid the Belgian draft. Disciplined, patient, mindful of his goal, Jacson was cautious, not asking to go inside the compound. He did small favors for the Trotskys and their friends, using his car to do errands or take people to the airport. In this way, he insinuated himself into the household much in the way Zborowski had gained the confidence of Lev Sedov.

By the spring of 1940 Trotsky was comfortable enough with the couple to invite them on a picnic accompanied by armed bodyguards. The attack in May put the compound on a heightened alert, but Trotsky refused to follow the security protocols that his guards devised. Jacson was allowed to enter the compound without being frisked. That August he asked Trotsky to review an essay he had written about political developments in France. Trotsky, always willing to assist a potential follower, agreed and welcomed Jacson into his study. For Jacson, this was a dress rehearsal. Trotsky was not impressed by the paper and expressed some frustration to his wife. A few days later, on August 20, Jacson returned to the compound. Although it was summer, he was dressed in a suit and an overcoat. Again, the guards did not search him. Jacson joined Trotsky in the courtyard, where Sedova noticed them near the rabbit cages. They then retired to the study.

*With the defeat of the Spanish Republic, more than a thousand veterans of the International Brigades took refuge in Mexico over the winter of 1939–1940. Trotsky had good reason to fear that their ranks included many committed Stalinists, any one of whom could be a potential assassin. Two, in fact, Siquerios and Mercader, attacked him.

Soon after, Sedova heard a terrible scream. She rushed to the study, followed by the guards, where they found Trotsky, blood streaming around his face, standing over the prostrate Jacson. Trotsky told them that Jacson had shot him with a revolver and urged the guards not to harm him so he could talk. Severely injured, Trotsky was losing strength and was soon lying on the floor. The mode of attack became clear. While Trotsky read his paper, Jacson moved behind his chair and plunged an ice axe into his skull, assuming that the blow would quickly and silently kill Trotsky. But the "old man" stood and jumped on Jacson, wrestling the axe from his hand and knocking him to the floor. This was how Sedova and the guards found them. Trotsky remained conscious and in control of himself. But he knew that the blow was fatal. "I feel that this time they succeeded," he told Sedova, tapping his chest.

Seva returned home from school at just that moment. He saw his grandfather on the floor before Sedova, lifting her gaze, noticed him and ordered the boy taken away. Trotsky had been working on his biography of Stalin that week. "Some of the manuscript of the unfinished portion was in Trotsky's study, strung out in enormously long strips of many sheets pasted end to end," his American translator Charles Malamuth wrote the following year. "In the struggle with the assassin portions of the manuscript were not only splattered with blood but utterly destroyed."

Trotsky was rushed to a hospital. When the nurses began to undress him, he asked his wife to do it herself. Still conscious, he expressed his love for her, then whispered, "Please say to our friends that I am sure of the victory of the Fourth International. Go forward." Those were his final words. Surgeons struggled for four hours to save him. But the axe had done its job, creating a deep wound in his cranium and brain. He succumbed the next day, twenty-six hours after the attack.

In the months before his death, Trotsky had affirmed his belief in revolution. "I shall die a proletarian revolutionist, a Marxist, a dialectical materialist, and, consequently, an irreconcilable atheist. My faith in the Communist future of mankind is not less ardent, indeed it is firmer today, than it was in the days of my youth." This unquestioning allegiance, after all the suffering he had inflicted and endured, constitutes the tragedy at the heart of Leon Trotsky's life: it had begun with contagious idealism and ended entangled in a murderous dream.

Epilogue

Saul Bellow was expecting to meet Trotsky on the day after the attack. He and his wife were visiting Mexico with another couple, and the two men had an appointment to see Trotsky that afternoon. At twenty-five, Bellow fancied himself a Trotskyist. His first short story had yet to appear in the *Partisan Review*. After learning about the attack, Bellow and his friend rushed to the hospital, where the police, thinking they were journalists, waved them into the room. There they saw Trotsky's corpse in an open coffin. "His cheeks, his nose, his beard, his throat, were streaked with blood and with dried iridescent trickles of iodine," Bellow recalled years later.

The assassination of Leon Trotsky stunned the world. Tens of thousands lined the streets of Mexico City, from curiosity as much as sympathy while the hearse wound its way through the crowds. Newspaper headlines announced his grisly end. In New York the *Times* acknowledged Trotsky's courage in the face of Stalin's relentless threats: He "knew who had killed him, and why. The long arm of Stalin's Ogpu had pursued him for years to Istanbul, to Norway, and at last to distant Mexico. It would have pursued him to the moon." But the tragedy of his death did not stop the *Times* from some irresponsible reporting. In the obituary, the *Times* claimed that Trotsky had been expelled from school at the age of fifteen for "desecrating a sacred icon, an image of the Russian Orthodox Church," and that his father had been a chemist. Both assertions were false. The obituary went on to claim—no doubt influenced by Walter Duranty—that when Trotsky was exiled to Turkey in January 1929, he "was preparing for a return to power by means of a revolution"; this was shabby coverage for such a major historical figure, however controversial. And in an editorial, eager to avoid sentimentality, the newspaper painted him as a "pathetic figure in his exile, his children dead, his money gone, his name reviled, his disciples shrunken to an oddly assorted band which called itself 'The Fourth International.'"

In Moscow, predictably, the Soviet press outdid itself with lies, proclaiming the "inglorious end" of a "murderer, traitor, and international spy." *Pravda* declared in the days following his death: "Trotsky, having gone to the limits of human debasement, became entangled in his own net and was killed by one of his disciples." This became the party line for decades.

Following his death, Trotsky's wife appealed to the U.S. government to permit his body to be taken to New York, where his followers could honor him. But the State Department refused. Trotsky was cremated, the ashes buried on the grounds of his final home, where a tall, imposing granite monument, decorated with a hammer and sickle, commemorates his memory only yards from where he was killed.

The Mexican police interrogated Frank Jacson, who was initially treated in the same hospital where Trotsky lay dying. Jacson, aka Jacques Mornard, aka Ramón Mercader, kept to his story and never divulged information about his political masters. He served a sentence of twenty years. According to a report in the *New York Herald Tribune*, during his first decade in prison he enjoyed "a luxurious carpeted apartment" with "a well-stocked library, a small kitchen where he can fix up snacks, and a private bedroom." His Mexican lawyer had been paying large sums to sustain his upkeep, funds that presumably originated in the Kremlin. Nonetheless, Mercader lived in constant terror, convinced that followers of Trotsky would find a way to take revenge or that agents of Stalin would silence him altogether; he physically attacked visitors and journalists who were brought to see him. But in early 1952 a new warden transferred a large group of privileged inmates, including Mercader, from their special quarters to regular cells. After his release in 1960, Mercader was first taken to Castro's Havana, then to Prague, and finally to Moscow, where, in a secret Kremlin ceremony, Leonid Brezhnev presented him with three major awards: Hero of the Soviet Union, the Order of Lenin, and the Gold Star. For the remainder of his life, Mercader divided his time between Havana and Moscow. He died in Cuba in October 1978 and was buried in Moscow. To this day, he has a place of honor in Russia's KGB Museum.

David Siquieros fared even better. It took Mexican police more than four months to catch up with him after his participation in the machine gun attack on Trotsky's compound. But when he was brought to trial, Siquieros turned on the court, accusing former President Cardenas of harboring a counterrevolutionary whose presence in the country had compromised Mexico's stability and security. Siquieros was acquitted of the major charges against him, including the murder of Robert Sheldon Harte and the attempted murder of Trotsky. President Manuel Ávila Camacho allowed him to avoid prison by leaving the country for Chile, but he returned to Mexico in early 1943 and lived there until his death in 1974; in death as in life, Mexico treated him as a national treasure.

It was Stalin, not Trotsky, who outlived his enemies. Ten months after Trotsky's death, Stalin—in the face of compelling intelligence that Hitler was planning an invasion—allowed the Wehrmacht to launch a surprise attack on the Soviet Union. But Moscow and its democratic allies prevailed in the end, leaving Stalin in control of Eastern Europe. Trotsky's prediction did not come to pass; Stalin and his regime survived the war, established the Warsaw Pact, and challenged the United States for political supremacy. Stalin died of natural causes in March 1953. Although his death shook the Kremlin, his heirs held on until 1991, when the Soviet Union followed the fate of its satellite regimes into the dustbin of history.

Trotsky's followers did not fare as well as his enemies. A week after the signing of the Molotov-Ribbentrop Pact in September 1939, Trotsky predicted that "the laboring masses will form a world Socialist federation of nations headed by the Fourth International to replace the present systems of governments." But the Fourth International was never more than a ramshackle collection of orthodox Marxists, now critical of Stalin, now defending his heirs. It is a history of continuous quarreling among fewer and fewer people, with each group asserting that it, above all others, understood Trotsky's philosophy and was therefore entitled to claim his mantle.

This writer once witnessed members of the Trotskyist Spartacist Youth confront the Soviet Ukrainian dissident Leonid Plyushch when he spoke at Harvard in the late 1970s; Brezhnev had forcibly confined Plyushch in a mental institution for his nonviolent activity. These young activists, so reverent of Trotsky and their understanding of the Bolshevik Revolution, could not acknowledge the simple truth of Plyushch's experience. In their own way, they were as detached from reality as their hero had been at times in his life. Even Natalia Sedova, who remained committed to preserving Trotsky's legacy, grew tired of his disciples' fervid attempts to make reality conform to their preconceived ideological notions. In 1950, when the leadership of the Fourth International hailed the Korean War as a fight against American imperialism, Sedova resigned from its Executive Committee. "I do not see his ideas in your politics," she wrote to them. There have been, however, serious-minded historians and political observers, like Isaac Deutscher, for whom Trotsky's rejection of Stalin helped to sustain their faith in Marxism and a commitment to overcome Stalin's burdensome legacy on the buried soul of socialism.

Stalin's heirs were also confounded by what to make of Trotsky. Under Mikhail Gorbachev's policy of *glasnost*, or greater openness, in the late 1980s, when the regime began to permit a more honest examination of Soviet history, it had difficulty coming to terms with Trotsky. His name was left out of the fourth edition of the *Soviet Encyclopedic Dictionary* in 1987, and Gorbachev himself, in his speech marking the seventieth anniversary of the revolution that November, asserted that after Lenin's death, Trotsky "displayed inordinate claims to leadership in the party, . . . denied the possibility of building socialism in conditions of capitalist encirclement, [while] in foreign policy [he and his followers] placed their faith in exporting revolution." Trotsky, in short, was "an excessively self-assured politician who always vacillated and cheated." It was not until January 1989 that Moscow's *Literaturnaya Gazeta* (Literary gazette) acknowledged that the Kremlin had been responsible for Trotsky's murder.

His political legacy may be weak today, but Trotsky continues to inhabit the popular imagination. George Orwell created the image of the "renegade and backslider" Emmanuel Goldstein—the principal enemy of Big Brother in *Nineteen Eighty-Four*—whose visage is projected onto screens throughout Oceania to provoke the hatred and fear of its citizens. Goldstein had been "one of the leading figures of the Party, almost on a level with Big Brother himself," but now he was the "primal traitor, the earliest defiler of the Party's purity. . . . All subsequent crimes against the Party, all treacheries, acts of sabotage, heresies, deviations, sprang directly out of his teaching." But Goldstein's writings still circulated secretly within the underground opposition, corrupting the life of Oceania as Stalin accused Trotsky of doing in Moscow.

Hollywood and the movies have not forgotten him. Richard Burton played him in 1972 in a film by Joseph Losey. The movie *Frida* highlights her affair with Trotsky. And in 2010 the Canadian feature film *The Trotsky* tells the story of a high school student who models his life and forays into school politics on the life of Leon Trotsky. Popular music groups in Europe recall him in their lyrics, most notably in the hit song "No More Heroes" by the British group the Stranglers and in "Jew and God" by the French *chanteur* Serge Gainsbourg, who describes a catalog of creative and revolutionary Jews from Jesus to Marx, Trotsky, and Einstein. Among literary works, Saul Bellow imagines the character Augie March (1953) happening upon Trotsky in a provincial Mexican city; Augie is soon asked to assume the role of Trotsky's nephew in a scheme to assure the "Old Man's" security. The American writer Isaac Rosenfeld describes an intense dream in his short story "The World of the Ceiling" (1956): a consumptive Trotsky, newly escaped from Siberia, hiding subversive leaflets from marauding Cossacks on a Russian street. Trotsky's time in New York is the basis for a chapter in the novel *End of the World News* (1983) by the British writer Anthony Burgess, and the American novelist Barbara Kingsolver places him in the Rivera-Kahlo household in Mexico City in *The Lacuna* (2009). Kingsolver has him tell one of the servants, "In 1917 I commanded an army of five million men. Now I command 11 hens."

Nearly a century after the Bolshevik Revolution and decades after his death, Leon Trotsky and the ideas that animated his life and career seem increasingly remote. The revolution he did so much to engineer collapsed under the weight of its historical legacy. We are left with the compelling image of a ruthless revolutionary, a brilliant journalist, an eloquent historian and pamphleteer, who never softened his faith in dogmatic Marxism, never questioned the need to use violent coercion as an instrument of historical progress, never wondered whether his dream of a proletarian dictatorship could really be the answer to every political, economic, and social failing.

His years in exile, his outspoken criticism of Stalin, the fate of his four children, and his own assassination deserve more than grudging sympathy. Harassed, threatened, virtually defenseless, Trotsky became an all-too-human figure as both Soviet and Western political leaders scorned him. Trotsky, in turn, never disavowed his vocation—to be a revolutionary. His courage and determination were as much the wellspring of his allure as they were the source of his undoing. Once removed from power, Trotsky was not as much of a threat to Stalin as either the Kremlin feared or his followers believed. But he refused to renounce the revolution that first betrayed, then destroyed him. He could not renounce himself.

NOTE ON SOURCES

I HAVE RELIED ON a host of primary material to explore the life and career of Leon Trotsky. He was a prolific writer, and no biography would be complete without careful attention to his memoir, *My Life;* his accounts of revolution, *1905* and *History of the Russian Revolution;* and his books on Lenin and Stalin. Trotsky's reporting on the Balkan Wars has been translated for the volume *The War Correspondence of Leon Trotsky: The Balkan Wars, 1912–1913*, edited by George Weissman and Duncan Williams. I was also privileged to spend many weeks in the Houghton Library of Harvard University, which holds a large archive of his papers, including letters and articles from the time of his exile, both to Alma Ata and then abroad. I consulted material in the archive of the YIVO Institute in New York. I also examined material in the Lavon Institute–Labour Archives and Library in Tel Aviv.

I would like to acknowledge my conversations with two people who actually knew Trotsky: his grandson Esteban Volkow welcomed me to the Trotsky Museum in Mexico City and graciously shared memories of his grandfather. I also met Lillian Pollak in New York; as a follower of Trotsky and a friend of the Ageloff sisters, she had visited him in Mexico in the late 1930s. They may be the last individuals with living memories of him.

There is a vast literature about Trotsky by people who knew him. Among these books, I would mention the account by G. A Ziv, *Trotskii: kharakteristika po lichnym vospominaniyam* (Trotsky: A character reference based on personal recollections); two by Max Eastman: *Leon Trotsky: The Portrait of a Youth* and *Since Lenin Died;* Victor Serge's *Memoir of a Revolutionary;* and the volume Serge edited with Trotsky's widow, Natalia Sedova, *The Life and Death of Leon Trotsky.*

In addition, I consulted a great deal of secondary literature, most notably the famous three-volume biography by Isaac Deutscher which appeared in the 1950s and 1960s. While Deutscher was a magnificent writer and carried out wide-ranging and unprecedented research, I regard his account as too forgiving of Trotsky's and Lenin's support for violent political repression when they wielded power. At other times, Deutscher's discussion of Trotsky's political acumen crosses the line into hagiography. I also take issue with Deutscher's evaluation of Stalin and his legacy. *The Social and Political Thought of Leon Trotsky,* by Baruch Knei-Paz, certainly the most exhaustive account of Trotsky's theoretical work, was a productive source of information. I found the work of Robert S. Wistrich, including his biography of Trotsky and his book *Revolutionary Jews,* particularly suggestive. Irving Howe's biography served as a kind of model of how to explore Trotsky's life and his work as a journalist and Marxist theoretician in a compact volume. It was also helpful to read other, more recent, accounts of Trotsky's life—by Joel Carmichael, Ian Thatcher,

Dmitri Volkogonov, Robert Service, and Bertrand Patenaude—
which were based on access to material that Deutscher could
not have seen. Though I do not always share their judgments—
Service, in particular, often engages in gratuitous criticism of
Trotsky's character and personality which I do not share and,
in my view, fails to understand the full complexity of Trotsky's
relationship to his Jewish origin—their work helped me to
gain greater understanding of aspects of his career. The volume
Trotsky and the Jews, by Joseph Nedava, provides a comprehensive review of material relating to Trotsky's relationship and
attitudes toward his origin and the challenges fellow Jews faced
during his lifetime. I often relied on this volume to point me in
one direction or another, though I often found myself disagreeing with Nedava on how to evaluate the material he discovered.
A master's thesis by Joseph Kester at Tel Aviv University about
Jewish themes in Trotsky's life (in Hebrew) also proved to be
useful, as did an undergraduate honors thesis by Leonard
Rubenstein, which he wrote at Wesleyan University.

There are innumerable accounts of the Russian Revolution
in English. I relied on the work of Adam Ulam, Alexander
Rabinowitch, Orlando Figes, Mikhail Heller, Alexander
Nekrich, and Rex Wade. I also consulted *Ten Days That Shook
the World*, by John Reed; *The Russian Revolution*, by Nikolai
Sukhanov; and *Stormy Passage*, by Wladimir Woytinsky; all
three men were in Petrograd in 1917 and watched Trotsky in
action at numerous historic moments.

A Russian-language volume entitled *Kniga Pogromov: Po-
gromy na Ukraine, v Belorussii i evropeyskoy chasti Rossii v period
Grazhdanskoy voiny 1918–1922* (The book of pogroms: Pogroms
in Ukraine, in Belorussia, and Jewish areas of Russia during the
period of the Civil War, 1918–1922; Moscow, 2007), edited by
L. B. Milyakova, proved to be a valuable reference about how
the image of Trotsky was used against vulnerable Jewish communities.

Lesley Chamberlain's book *Lenin's Private War: The Voyage of the Philosophy Steamer and the Exile of the Intelligentsia* provides important information about Trotsky's attitude toward independent intellectuals in Russia; Elizabeth A. Wood of the Massachusetts Institute of Technology and a colleague at Harvard's Davis Center for Russian and Eurasian Studies referred me to her book *The Baba and the Comrade: Gender and Politics in Revolutionary Russia*, where she discusses Trotsky's writings about Russian habits and ordinary life; *Intimate Enemies: Demonizing the Bolshevik Opposition, 1918–1928*, by Igal Halfin, reveals little-known examples of how Trotsky and others were harassed; Gennady Estraikh of New York University alerted me to incidents in the life of Abe Cahan and the *Forverts* that were connected to Trotsky's career; and Dr. Henry Cohen shared an article from *Esquire* about Trotsky's attitude toward waiters in New York. Pavel Ilyin was kind enough to offer me information about the renaming of cities and towns in honor of Soviet leaders. Maxim Shrayer of Boston College alerted me to a poem in Trotsky's honor by Trotsky's cousin Vera Inber.

Terry Brotherstone and Paul Dukes edited *The Trotsky Reappraisal*, which includes many entries worth consulting, including an essay by Trotsky's nephew, Valery Bronstein, about the fate of their relatives under Stalin.

An essay by William Chase entitled "Trotsky in Mexico: Toward a History of His Discreet Contacts with the U.S. Government (1937–1940)" appeared in Russian in *Otechestvennaya istoriya* (Native history; issue no. 4, 1995); it explores hitherto unknown attempts by Trotsky to enter the United States.

During my research, I looked over back issues of the *New York Times*, the *Nation*, the *New Republic*, *Pravda*, and *Izvestia*, as well as consulting numerous scholarly articles in a host of journals.

ACKNOWLEDGMENTS

I AM PARTICULARLY GRATEFUL to Anita Shapira and Steven J. Zipperstein, the editors of the Jewish Lives series, for offering me the challenge of writing of this book. Their counsel and judgment helped orient me as I navigated my way through a difficult thicket of history and personality. Ileene Smith and Sarah Miller of Yale University Press were also encouraging as I approached the finish line. Ronald Aronson of Wayne State University and Susan Weissman of St. Mary's College read the manuscript and offered serious, well-informed criticism and suggestions, as did my friends Boris Katz and Susanna Kaysen. They all did their best to convince me of where I might be going wrong, and for the most part I took their advice.

As always, I am grateful to be associated with Harvard's Davis Center for Russian and Eurasian Studies, where ongoing discussions and interaction with colleagues prove to be invaluable. I am also privileged to have access to Widener Library, where the Slavic librarian Luba Dyky has been a true friend. The staff of Harvard's Houghton Library, which houses the Trotsky Archive, was invariably patient and well informed in response to my endless requests for documents. And my colleagues at Amnesty International USA demonstrated their support when they granted me a sabbatical leave in the early stages of the project.

My agent, Robin Straus, once again expressed more than a mere professional enthusiasm for the book. And my wife, Jill Janows, and our son, Ben, continued to exhibit fortitude and understanding as I took on the work of research and writing.

INDEX

JEWISH LIVES is a major series of interpretive
biography designed to illuminate the imprint of eminent Jewish
figures upon literature, religion, philosophy, politics, cultural and
economic life, and the arts and sciences. Subjects are paired with
authors to elicit lively, deeply informed books that explore the
breadth and complexity of Jewish experience
from antiquity through the present.

Jewish Lives is a partnership of Yale University Press
and the Leon D. Black Foundation.

Historians Anita Shapira and Steven J. Zipperstein
are series editors.